David

Olwyn Harris

Reflections on a shepherd boy
who becomes king and the forefather of Messiah

Suitable for Individual and Group Discussion

Copyright © Olwyn Harris 2025

ISBN   Softcover   978-1-923021-34-1
       eBook   978-1-923021-35-8

All rights reserved. No part of this book may be reproduced or transmitted in any form or by any means, electronic, or mechanical, including photocopying, recording or by any information storage and retrieval system without the permission in writing by the copyright owner.
Unless otherwise stated Scriptures quoted here are from the King James Version (Authorised version). First published in 1611. Quoted from the KJV Classic Reference Bible, copyright 1983 by the Zondervan Corporation.

Published by: Reading Stones Publishing
Helen Brown & Wendy Wood
Woodwendy1982.wixsite.com/readingstones
Cover Design: Olwyn Harris. Some of the cover elements were created using AI Technology.

For more copies contact the publisher at:

Glenburnie
212 Glenburnie Road
ROB ROY NSW 2360
Mobile: 0422 577 663
Email: Readingstonespublishing@gmail.com

Acknowledgement:

My heartfelt appreciation to Pastor Dawn Peel, emeritus, who has held a role supporting the credentialling of pastors within the Australian Christian Churches Movement. Thank you for your willingness to cast your theological eye over these chapters.

Table of Contents

David

Table of Contents ____ 5
Introduction ____ 7
A Devoted Heart ____ 9
A Warriors Heart ____ 24
A Faithful Heart ____ 40
A Refreshed Heart ____ 53
An Offended Heart ____ 69
A Wounded Heart ____ 83
A Worshipping Heart ____ 97
A Forgiving Heart ____ 113
A Repentant Heart ____ 127
A Humble Heart ____ 140
A Prophetic Heart ____ 155
Endnotes ____ 169

Introduction

Taking time to reflect on the stories in the Bible, is something that we are encouraged to do in our walk with Jesus. I don't know anyone who would suggest this is not an important aspect of being a disciple of Jesus. Yet I have noticed, over and over, there is a widespread illiteracy regarding the stories in the Bible which I grew up with. I've also noticed that this unfamiliarity is not restricted to new Christians. I suspect we are more comfortable with the popular narratives on our TV streaming service, than the ones in our Bible.

The Holy Spirit, in his wisdom, has chosen the platform of storytelling as one way to communicate our spiritual relationship with him, packed with wisdom, truth, morality, and values. It is not the only way God speaks to us, yet so much practical wisdom can be distilled from these narratives. Our challenge is how to access these stories in a way that allows them to be understandable in a world that is so far removed from the times when these accounts occurred. This series on *Reflections in the Bible* is not intended to be an exercise in theological exegesis, rather to create an opportunity to explore some of these stories. It is an invitation to go on a journey of reflection around what is described. What can we distil from these life-stories that makes sense for us today? Some of these narratives may be familiar. Some of them may be forgotten. Some of them are hard to understand. This is an opportunity to take time to slow down, invite the Holy Spirit to whisper his insight as we explore some of the stories he has preserved for us.

This book is intended to be a reflective space to use alongside your Bible. Sometimes, even the act of opening the pages of our Bible can be a challenge. So, open up! Don't skip over the suggested passages marked as "Bible Readings". The scriptures tagged as "Bible Reference" are intended to bookmark passages, if you want to check them. Take hold of the opportunity to read or revisit God's Word. You are invited to use these pages as a place to scribble in margins; explore your own questions; and use reflective prompts to go a little deeper. My prayer is that it will be a springboard to explore the incredible love story of God, his great good news of redemption and His grace will draw you closer to who He is as our Good Father. I trust it moves each of us to appreciate more about our relationship with God, ourselves and life in community.

I

A Devoted Heart

This series of reflections is on the life of David, who is perhaps the most famous king of Israel. He is identified as the great King of Israel King whose linage leads directly to Jesus as Israel's Messiah. There is so much recorded about the life of David, that it is difficult to choose where to focus our thoughts. With that in mind, there are many accounts of David's story that we may not consider in detail, but it is good reading, and I encourage you to go through the Books of Samuel... and look at the events of David's life.

So, let's start our journey where we first meet David, and it is not in a place you would expect to find the next King of Israel, nor is it a place where one might think is appropriate for one who would become the forefather of Messiah.

Some background...

The prophet Samuel was recognised as the last of the great Judges of Israel, and the Israelite people demanded that Samuel instate a monarchy like the nations around them. So, on God's instructions, Samuel anoints a man from the tribe of Benjamin. Saul was selected by God to be the first King of Israel. Saul's reign started strong. He was a humble man, and he worked at removing the shame that their servitude to the oppressive nations around them created; he won many battles against the Philistines. However, after some time, this changes. The pressure to people-please takes its toll on King Saul. In fact, things changed so much that Saul was no longer taking responsibility for his disobedient choices but blames those around him. He killed prophets if he didn't like what they said, and King Saul becomes defensive, paranoid, and fickle.

The irony is that the people of Israel wanted a king like those of the nations around them, and now, that is exactly what they had. But God had a different plan.

God spoke to Samuel and told him that in the spiritual realm, God had already removed King Saul from the throne of Israel... but that was still to be outworked on the ground. So, Samuel removed himself from Saul's presence completely. Now, in his old age, Samuel has nothing to do with Saul again while he was alive.

God's plan was to have a king who was *not* like the nations around them, but to have a king who was aligned with His heart. A king who carried the Spirit of God, a king who is good and merciful, with a heart that worships, and has the capacity to not give up fighting for what is right. That is what God wanted reflected in His King.

So, let's look at the beginning of the account where we meet David for the first time in Scripture.

Bible Reading
1 Samuel 16: 1-5

God is doing a new thing...

King Saul was making choices that grieved Samuel. So much so that he had not just withdrawn from the King's court, but from all public life and was in a protracted period of mourning. Yet here God was very specifically inviting Samuel to do something very public.

What is the specific thing that God asked Samuel to do? (verse 1)

Yet Samuel is reluctant. This is a realistic picture we are presented with. This was not a small thing that God was asking of him. Samuel immediately recognises that this commission could mean his death. King Saul's reputation was now one of being punitive and vindictive. It is apparent that Saul had made it clear that he will not tolerate any threat to his throne. Samuel could not just go and anoint a new King over Israel.

There is something in Samuel's devotion as he re-engages in public life that I find inspiring. He is now an old man; he is 89 years old. Samuel had been dedicated as a Nazarite… even before he was born. This was a vow that involved a number of commitments to set his life apart dedicated to the service of God; one of those was that his hair would never be cut. Now his hair is grey, probably thinned and wispy, most likely tied up in a turban. He is walking along the road into Bethlehem, he might be hobbling, maybe a little stooped, perhaps using a staff to give him stability. He has with him a sacrificial heifer, leading her by a halter along the road. His anointing horn slung over his shoulder, maybe concealed by his cloak. There is nothing about this picture that looks like a spiritual upheaval, or a political move against the reigning monarch.

God chooses unlikely instruments to accomplish the things of the Kingdom of God. God does not discard Samuel just because he is aged or because Saul had no use for him.

I like to think that Samuel's reluctance had nothing to do with doubt, or disobedience, or even just caution… but just a practical *"how?"* How could he actually do this? How could he obey God without this becoming a bloodbath? How could he do this without having the whole house of Jesse massacred? Which would mean himself and his own family included in that number?

Did you notice that the elders of Bethlehem react very strongly when Samuel arrives? The sudden reappearance of Samuel must have been shocking for them. Samuel had been out of public office for a long time. King Saul had been reigning for 27 years when Samuel suddenly appears in Bethlehem. They knew the prophet Samuel was estranged from King Saul. Young men from their village had been conscripted into Saul's army. Perhaps they were worried Samuel had arrived to take revenge on their support of Saul as their King. Yet they obviously respect Samuel's office and honour his position as prophet and judge, even in the current political climate.

Samuel reassures them... "I'm here to offer a sacrifice... I'm here to worship." We see Samuel confidently step back into the office of judge and prophet under God's authority, and he invites the people of Bethlehem to the sacrificial meal. He publicly steps out of the shadows and obeys what God has laid on his heart.

As Samuel offers that sacrificial heifer, I wonder if he had any prophetic insight into the fact that it would be in Bethlehem where Messiah would be born? Did he understand that this public appearance was an outpouring of God's grace towards a larger plan? God was unveiling the next part of His plan of Redemption, a plan of Restoration, a plan of Salvation.

That plan was not just for David, not just for the house of Jesse, not just for Israel, but this was an announcement for all humanity. It would be here in Bethlehem, from the line of David, where Jesus the Messiah, would be born.

Bible Reading
1 Samuel 16:5-13

Samuel – Anointing God's choice

This was a good-looking family. They were positioned, prosperous and had a distinguished feel about them.

The eldest son, Eliab, had that look about him – the look of a king. Saul had that same royal distinguished bearing when he was anointed. This was the type of person God had anointed last time, surely God would do the same thing again.

But God was not going for the people's choice this time.
    Eliab... no
    Abinadab... no
    Shammah... no
Samuel went through the seven sons that Jesse presented.

What is God looking for? (verse 7)

Am I easily impressed by the distinguished externals?

All these men were strong, respected men of their community, yet there was something in their heart that did not measure up. I have struggled with the transliteration of the word "rejected" because the connotations this word has for me are things like *discarded, worthless, of no use*. Yet God was not a rejecting them as people, but he knew they were not the right people for *this* role.

Later, we see David's brothers join him in the wilderness when he is hiding to escape King Saul's bounty on his head. They fight with David and after he is crowned King these men make a significant contribution to the Kingdom of Israel, particularly in the military. They are still sons of Israel; they still have a contribution to make... but *not* in the role as king.

Samuel is here specifically looking for the individual whom God was going to anoint as the next King of Israel.

One of the roles I used to hold was working as a community nurse, visiting clients in their homes. I remember visiting an aboriginal man who had a diving accident when he jumped off a bridge into a river. As a result of that trauma, he was a quadriplegic. I met him as a patient who was bedridden, had very little mobility, was very dependent on his family and professionals for care. My role was to come in and dress some of the ulcers that were a result of his mobility issues. We got along quite well, and he taught me many things about his culture. During the time I was visiting him, I remember one night waking up from a powerful dream that I knew was a vision from God. I saw this man standing on a rocky outcrop. He was holding traditional spears and implements, standing tall and strong on one leg, resting the other on his knee. In the vision he had all the scarring across his chest and arms that he described to me were the medallions of battles and victories won. I heard the voice of Jesus speak words over him.

What challenged me, was that I saw this person one way, and yet God saw him another way completely. God did not look at externals of a person dependent and unable to move, but God was seeing his heart. This man had the heart of a fighter. God saw him as a warrior.

In a sense, these young men were eliminated from the presidential race. They were denied *this* particular role. God was not going to anoint and appoint someone on the basis of their distinguished bearing. Scripture tells us it was on the basis of his **heart** that God anointed and appointed David.

David – the Shepherd

I have been so curious as to why David is out in the paddocks working like a hired hand. This is a distinguished and influential family. Jesse is a respected and esteemed man in the community of Bethlehem. It suggests to me that this dismissal of David is more than just allocating someone to do the chores. A family of this standing had many hired men, and yet David was being treated like one of them... a hired hand. He is about 15 years old, but he is not being treated like a son.

When Samuel asks Jesse's sons to be presented to him, his older sons are all that Jesse offers. David is dismissed. So much so, he is not even considered in the line-up, but we are only given a few hints in scripture as to why that was.

Am I dismissive of things that don't seem all that impressive?

Bible Reading
Psalm 69: 8,12,19

A few years ago, I went on a trail exploring what was known about David's mother and why we know so little about her... not even her name is mentioned in scripture. We know she is only referred to, once or twice in David's psalms, which I thought was sort of odd given he is the most famous of the Hebrew Kings. So, that suggested to me there was a story in the silence.

When I explored some Hebrew traditions, I found that a story that [i]went something like this:

Jesse married a Jewess named Nitzevet. Jesse was a highly respected religious and community man who presided over the Sanhedrin in their community. It is believed that after their first seven sons were born, his sons were also highly esteemed and favoured in the community.
However, Jesse went through a period of deep self-doubt, where he questioned his legitimacy as a Jew because his grandmother – Ruth, was a Moabitess, and his great grandmother, Rahab was a gentile from Jericho. Jewish men by Mosaic law were forbidden to inter-marry with gentiles. Jesse interpreted the law to mean that to marry a Jewess, when he was an illegitimate convert to Judaism, meant that he was living in sin, and so he voluntarily separated from his wife Nitzevet. The family knew about this decision.
If this was the case, and he had married illegitimately, in Jesse's mind, the rightful inheritance of his sons also came under question. After a period of separation, he intensely desired to have a legitimate heir to secure his inheritance. According to Jesse's thinking, as a converted gentile, he could marry a converted gentile-woman, but not a Jewess. So, taking the example of Abraham who married Hagar, the gentile handmaiden of Sarah, he decided to take Nitzevet's handmaiden as his wife, who was a Canaanite.
What Jesse didn't count on was the loyalty and faithfulness that this servant-woman had for his estranged wife. The handmaiden went to Nitzevet and explained Jesse's plan and proposed that they swap places

like Leah and Rachel did on Jacob's wedding night, without Jesse knowing. They did this and Nitzevet conceived and becomes pregnant with David. However, now that Nitzevet is pregnant, her dilemma was whether she would expose her husband or be accused of infidelity herself. She chooses to remain silent, even when her other son's demand her death as an adulterer. Jesse intervenes and saves her life; however, she was to be ostracised, and her baby treated as an illegitimate slave.

Read the words of Psalm 69 again with this context in mind. Does it add depth to his words? David knew about shame; he knew about disgrace, just as his mother did. It is possible that this psalm was expressing David's very real experience and was not just poetic license when he was having a bad day. Perhaps David really did know about *disgrace...* and also God's *grace*. Profoundly.

Shepherding was considered an unclean occupation. Perhaps it seemed reasonable that this role be given to David, who was considered by the family as no more than a bastard servant boy. There was no younger son favouritism occurring here. There is no doting father like the patriarch Jacob who doted on his son Joseph. David's older brothers were not jealous of him – they were ashamed of him. His brothers considered David illegitimate scum, less than nothing. Where others saw David as an embarrassment and a disgrace, God saw him as a king.

What steps could I take to see others more as God sees them?

In this tradition, Nitzevet had no public recognition of her decision to do what she thought was the right thing. David grew up with no public profile, except that of a bastard. He was scorned. It makes sense that David wasn't included when Samuel summons Jesse's sons. David wasn't even on Jesse's radar, because Jesse didn't consider him a legitimate son. David was an embarrassment, and certainly not worthy to be presented to the visiting prophet Samuel.

I have shared this story surrounding the controversy of this tradition regarding David's mother, Nitzevet, to acknowledge that even in the *tradition,* there is a reminder that God looks at our heart. Whether this is actually part of the story of David's family or not, it becomes a reminder that God is not moved by public opinion and popular profiles, tainted histories or the shame of controversy. God was not looking at externals. God was not even looking for respectable, or distinguished. The choice of David was not about how good-looking he was or how fine he would look on the cover of "Mighty Men" Magazine. We are told that David was handsome and later, as a celebrity warrior, the dancing girls swooned. But before all that, when there were no external qualities, or family status, that would recommend him to anyone... when no one else noticed... God saw David. Even when he had no standing in the community, no reputation, no prestige; he had a common, lowly job and the opinions of others were pretty scathing. David was dismissed, but God saw what no one else could see: God saw all the potential that he had created in him.

What things do you see that is a pattern of Messiah in this story?

The Pattern of Messiah

The prophet Isaiah wrote this about Messiah:

Bible Reading
Isaiah 53: 2-3

God takes what is dismissed by others and makes something remarkable in the Kingdom of God when hearts are aligned with his purposes. It was a pattern that was bearing witness to Messiah... right at the beginning of his royal lineage. Right from the start. God could see David's heart. He saw there was resilience there, a devoted heart.

What do you think David was doing while he was out in the paddocks?

I think he was working, caring for the sheep; attending to their needs; providing pasture and water. He was learning to master his skill as a warrior, protecting sheep from predators, lions and bears, becoming skilled with the slingshot. He was learning to master the harp as a musician, craft his words as a poet and a psalmist. He was learning to pray and hear God's word.

In his sermon to the synagogue at Perga, Paul summarises God's appointment of David.

Bible Reading
Acts 13: 22
1 Samuel 2:35

Did you notice that God declares there is no illegitimacy here? David *is* the son of Jesse and (even more importantly) he has the internal love and motivation to do everything God wanted him to do.

Faithlessness was Saul's sin. He only went part way; he didn't wholeheartedly do what God asked of him. He only managed to do his own version of what God wanted. King Saul justified and spiritualised his disobedience. He was never willing to be fully accountable.

Samuel was tempted to consider the polished, distinguished externals. Regardless of the reasons why, Jesse dismissed David and was not even able to acknowledge him as his own son. Yet, in the face of rejection, pain, heartache and prejudice David chose to stay sweet and soft in the face of adversity. He chose to keep on faithfully walking with God; walking in the identity of who God had created them to be; doing what God had put in his hand to do at each season of his life, even if it was keeping sheep safe by fighting off bears or lions.

Bible Reference
1 Samuel 2:35 19:18

The word of God came to Eli the priest, who led Israel as Judge, before Samuel. God was looking for a priest who would do according to what was is in God's heart and mind. Another way to read that might be, "I will raise up a priest who is a man after my own heart and mind…" The same idea is reflected in David's story. God is looking at hearts. David and Samuel were two men from different generations who had a heart after God own heart. Saul's heart imploded into a narcissistic, paranoid, obsessive track.

When things get challenging, where does my heart go?

Samael's heart stayed honourable and soft in the face of adversity, heartache and prejudice. David's heart, even as a young person, was learning to faithfully walk with God; learning to hear, learning to worship and learning to fight for those in his care, which at his point, were his father's sheep. David is walking in the identity of who God had created him to be. David is doing what God had put in his hand to do, even if his family could not acknowledge his worth.

Is my heart honourable, and soft, and worshipful, regardless of how others see me?

If God is looking at my heart, what does He see?

Final Thoughts...

If we follow the timeline of these stories...
Saul was 57 years old when Samuel anointed David.
David was about 15 years old.
It will be *another* 15 years before David becomes king in Hebron and David isn't crowned king in Jerusalem over all of Israel until 7 years after that, when he was 37 years old.

It is worth noting God is not a microwave God. But he is a God who works thoroughly in hearts. Samuel grieved the changes in King Saul that were not the ways of a Godly king. But God invites Samuel to fill up his horn and he sends him to the house of Jesse. God is not impressed with the distinguished externals. God is not influenced by public opinion or tarnished backgrounds.

When we were on a holiday in Florence, Italy, we went to see the original Michelangelo's sculpture of David. The tour-guide told us that the block of marble Michelangelo chose to work with was rejected by many other sculptors because it had too many seams and flaws to be any good... or so they thought. They believed they needed something flawless to make something of significant beauty. Under the right hand, the flaws did not disqualify the material from becoming a masterpiece. Michelangelo was commissioned to carve this piece, as one of many sculptures that would be positioned on the facade of a building in one of the main city squares, as was common practice during this Renaissance period. So apart from the detail, that for a Jew this portrayal of David has him very much intact and not circumcised, it is an incredible masterpiece of art. It was understood that no one would ever see the back of the sculpture when it was in place on the building, so the detail for the back of the piece was not considered important. Yet Michelangelo masterfully worked the detail on every aspect of the sculpture. Front and back and this sculpture has become one of the world's most visited, most scrutinised works of art in history.

I think of the life of David as a masterpiece as well. David was born a 'nobody'. No one ever thought anyone would see the work behind the scenes, yet David's life has been one of the most probed and studied and explored characters in our Scripture. David didn't just polish the visible aspects of his life, but he worked on those things in his heart, the behind the scenes, the hidden parts, just as much as the visible parts and this is what makes the difference.

What can I do differently that will better guard the spiritual health of my heart?

This is what takes an ordinary man and makes it a masterpiece under the hand of God. The difference is his heart. It is the health and nature of our heart that determines whether we step into all that God has for us, or whether we are left to stagnate, or worse... deteriorate into corruption. God looks into our heart and sees us.

Prayer:

Father God, thank you that you are a God who sees all of me. You see the visible; and you see the hidden places. Father, regardless of what other people think, you are a God who doesn't look at the seams and the flaws and then discard me. Thank you that use those materials and transform my life into the work of something remarkable, because under your hand the seams and the flaws are not a problem, rather they become part of the beauty of the finished work.
I ask Father God, that you would help me to look after the health of my heart. Give me eyes to see what you see... help me to see the people I come across this week as you see them. Help me to attend diligently to where I am positioned in this season and continue to align me with what you are doing... in my family, workplace, social circle, and community... now and into the future.
In Jesus' name, Amen.

2

A Warriors Heart

Where we are...

We were introduced to David when Samuel anointed him as a fifteen-year-old, as the designated next king of Israel. This was a bold announcement that God's plan was to have a king who was different from the nations around them... a king who carried the spirit of God. His Holy Spirit is good, and merciful. God wanted a king with a heart that worships, that reflected his goodness, his mercy, a heart with the capacity to not give up fighting for what is right.

So, what happens after Samuel anoints David and goes back to Ramah? Nothing. Not immediately. David returns to looking after his father's sheep. He does not know when that transition from the sheep-pens to the king's court will occur. Then towards the end of Chapter 16, we are told that King Saul begins to be tormented by dark moods. Saul would have episodes that tormented him, and nothing would offer him relief. The advice given, was to find a skilled musician who could sooth him with music and song. Someone had heard David play the harp and recommended him: a door opens. So, David was seconded to the king's court to serve. He would play and sing, and without fail, Saul's dark episodes would lift.

David was a likeable young man. Saul promoted him to his personal staff. He also became one of the king's armour bearers. Close, personal, trusted. It could seem that this remarkable random choice of a musician was a providential way to pick a shepherd up out of the paddocks and position him close to the king. Would this be the way God would position and promote David? Perhaps. He's in the royal court now... so it would not be a difficult thing for him to continue on and up, until he has the main job. We don't know how long this arrangement with Saul went on, but we know that David toggled back and forth between being at home with Jesse his father, looking after sheep, and being in service with the king. And then... war breaks out with their Philistine neighbours again... and life is thrown into turmoil once more.

This was a reoccurring theme, during Saul's reign. Over and over as the kingdom of Israel was stabilising, Saul had to defend their boarder against their warlike tribal neighbours. There were four major wars that had occurred prior to this, during Saul's reign. Wars that he won. King Saul was a veteran fighter. He knew how it was done. This particular conflict was with the Philistines... again. They had faced them before. But this time there is a different approach that was been taken by them.

Bible Reading
1 Samuel 17:1-11

There are three main figures in this story:
King Saul – the ruler of the Israelites
Goliath – the champion warrior of the Philistines
David – a shepherd, who was not even conscripted into the army like his three older brothers.

Was Saul willing to stand?
This is a very intimidating situation. This was a situation where the Israelites were called out to stand to face an unwinnable contest. They challenged any man to stand, in a one-on-one contest.

Bible Reference
1 Samuel 9:2

If you are looking for a champion to face a giant of a man, who would you choose from the ranks of the Israelites? Possibly you would look for someone with a strong physique. When Saul was chosen to be king, he stood head-and-shoulders above those around him. He was a big man; he was a warrior with experience. This made him the logical choice. Yet in this situation – he is afraid for his life and his kingdom. There is lot at stake, and he is terrified. He was unwilling, even unable to stand against this threat.

Where was Saul's confidence?

Saul was appointed by God to lead his nation into freedom from oppression from those nations around him. Even though he has been told by Samuel that God had transferred the royal line to another man, and he would not hand over the royal batten to his son, Saul, in this moment, was still king. This was still his mandate. Even with his battle experience and an army behind him, Saul is very much alone in this fight. His past experiences hold no water here. He has lost faith. He has lost confidence.

The only strategy Saul engages was to "buy" a champion: perhaps he could persuade someone to step up. He throws out incentives of reward money; perks such as marriage into the royal family; promises that their entire family would be exempt from taxes. All this, including steak knives, if someone would step up to the battle line. And still, no one moves.

Where do I put my confidence?

What estimation did Saul make of the enemy?

As Saul assesses this situation, he did not underestimate the hand of the Philistines, and he did not underestimate the hand of Goliath. This experienced warrior was holding all the cards. Like the Israelites spying out the promised land, their side looked like grasshoppers in his eyes. He was not able to take the stories of their heritage, or the experiences of Joshua and Caleb and find the reassurance that God was bigger than even this giant.

Which lens do I use when I make an estimation of a situation?

Who was Saul listening to?

Saul was listening to the sound of the camp. He believed what everyone else believed: that defeat is inevitable. He was listening to his fear, and to Goliath's intimidation and the result was that he lost heart.

Bible Reading
1 Samuel 17:12-43

Was Goliath willing to stand?

Goliath was arrogant, Oh yes! Goliath was very much in. He had this covered! He was a champion; he was a warrior – he was *raised* to be a fighter. He had experience – not just brute strength, he had that too.

He revels in the role of being a bully and he revels taking on the role of hero. Goliath was arrogant.

Where was Goliath's confidence?

Goliath believed in himself... and not without reason. His imposing height was six cubits and a span. A cubit was 18 inches in measurement, so Goliath was over 9 feet tall... about 3 metres. He was massive! A hulk! This was not his first picnic. He had warfare experience. He had extraordinary physical strength and impressive battle armour. He was set. Confidence was high.

Where do I put my confidence?

What estimation did Goliath make of the enemy?

Goliath estimation of this situation is one sided and arrogant. He could taste the Israelites fear. He very much underestimated David. "Do you think I'm a dog, that you are going to beat me off with a stick?" He very much underestimated the God of Israel. He cursed David with the names of his own gods and dismissed the stories he had heard about the God of Israel. That was historical, and it didn't apply to now.

Who was Goliath listening to?

Goliath was listening to the sound of *his* camp; everyone on his side of the fence was convinced that victory was inevitable. He was also listening to the panic in Israel's army and the result was a hard and arrogant heart.

At one time I was part of a Christian theatre group. This creative ministry had lots of opportunities to engage in community events and use this medium to share the love of Jesus. It was fun, it was gentle, it was boisterous, and we had a lot of great times working together. We would minister to both adults and children... at community events, in schools, churches, retreats and workshops. One event we attended, was a community fair. I was in character as a clown named "Sondrop", doing street work, blessing people and making them smile. It was a big day; my kids were also taking part and by lunchtime we were done. We needed to go home.

There is a rule when you are doing this kind of ministry, that if you are in costume, you stay in character. And when you are in character, you don't do normal things, like go and collect the mail. I broke the 'rule'. I went to get some things at the grocery shop for lunch before we went home.

I'm in the shopping centre with my kids, in costume, when one of the grocery store staff pushing a big stock trolley ran over my daughter's foot. So, I'm there... trying to look credible as a mother in a clown costume, (that didn't work), and I am aware that my daughter now has a significant injury. So, out goes the clown and I'm totally in mum mode. A lady witnessed the whole thing and took me aside and told me to make sure that I have it all recorded properly and wouldn't allow them to fob me off. I speak with the staff, trying to get them to understand that I needed an incident report done; I needed witnesses recorded; I needed a timeline captured. But they did fob me off. The reality of it is that if you're dressed as a clown, you don't have a lot of credibility with anyone, much less corporate organisations.

Over the next few weeks, I went back... and I went back... and I went back... to the manager of the store. I requested that they honour their verbal agreement that physiotherapy for my daughter would be paid for by them. I could see her dream of dancing was being jeopardised. When you come up against a big supermarket corporation as a housewife from a country town, it feels like you are up against a giant. Their legal department was sending me letters accusing me of being an irresponsible parent; and that my children were running wild. If it had been any one of my other children, I might have entertained the idea, but my gentle eldest daughter was not like that. The report that they did on the day to appease me was not recorded adequately and omitted vital details so that in the end it was effectively worthless.

As I sat down to write another letter, I paused and prayed, and I asked God to help me discern what was the outcome that I really wanted. What did I want? Two things: To have my daughter's physiotherapy treatment paid for because financially that would have been difficult for us to manage. And that this injury would have no lasting impact on my daughter's love for dancing.

God answered that prayer. The corporation agreed to meet the costs of the physiotherapy that my daughter might need... (without acknowledging any fault of course, as the incident occurred because of my inability to restrain my children!). My daughter has continued to dance. She achieved her teacher's qualification in dance and into adulthood she is still enjoying dancing and passing on that love of dance to others. It has been a big part of blessing in her life.

What are the Goliaths in my life that are intimidating me?

Bible Reading
1 Samuel 17: 33-49

Was David willing to stand?

David was Assured. David's brother, Eliab, saw his brother as an arrogant upstart, walking around the camp big noting himself. But I notice that this is David's way of making it known that he was willing to step forward. A visiting shepherd doesn't just present himself to the king. He has to be invited. I don't believe David's motivation was ever about the tax perks. Someone overheard David asking questions and reported it to King Saul.

David wanted to defend God's name and remove the shame and humiliation that the situation was imposing. David saw what no one else in the camp saw. The Philistines were not offering a one-on-one challenge. They were insulting God! How dare they! And something rose up inside of David that he could not let pass.

Was David conceited, arrogant and proud, as Eliab accused him of being? After all he was just there to deliver the pizza (the bread and cheese) and then he was supposed to go back and return to his duties at home. David has no battlefield experience, but he is not unfamiliar to engaging with the big and the fierce. His past experiences have prepared him for this. Lions and bears are the giants of the shepherds' world. Wisely David does it his way, he doesn't try to wear Saul's unfamiliar armour. He has faith that God who having held him strong in those other situations, would hold him here. He has confidence but that is not arrogance.

What estimation did David make of the enemy?

David did not underestimate the hand of Goliath; he wasn't flippant about this, but he had not underestimated the lion or the bear either. He knew that the history of Israel demonstrated over and over, that God is bigger, even bigger than a giant.

Am I willing to stand?

Who was David listening to?

David was a young man whose job was a shepherd. Yes, he was anointed by God to place of headship as king in the future, but that time was not now. He was still shepherding sheep and sometimes required to be on Saul-duty, to sooth him with music and song. Technically, this was not his fight. His call to lead his nation into freedom from the oppression imposed by those nations around him, was not part of his brief... yet. But right now, as David hears the insults from the enemy and the fear of those around him, and he cannot let it go. He *refuses* to let it go!

Who am I listening to?

David was not listening to the fear of the camp; he was not listening to the insults from his oldest brother. He was not listening to the arrogance of the enemy. He did not believe what everyone else believed... that defeat was inevitable; that the philistines would win this battle. He was listening to his heart, and to the stirring of the Holy Spirit that this situation was so wrong, on so many levels, and this was the right thing to fight for. There was a grating sound that was not congruent with the Kingdom of God and that is what he was going to address. The result was that his warrior's heart shone through, even when he wasn't officially a soldier.

What holds me back from making a stand?

Bible Reading
1 Samuel 17:50-58

Don't you love the question Saul asks Abner, his commander: "Whose son is he?" Regardless of David being regularly in King Saul's court; regardless that David was always on call to soothe Saul's agitation and his dark episodes with music and song; regardless of being a bi-vocational shepherd and an armour bearer for the king. It seems that this question reveals that David was never really seen by Saul. Not really. Hebrews live and breathe linage. It is how they know who you are and where you fit into the scheme of things. Practically, this information would be required if Saul was going to dispense the tax-perks he had promised to the victor and his family. Saul didn't know any of this regarding David. His insular, self-absorbed kingship is showing.

David might not have been seen until now. But *now* David is visible. An event of this magnitude means he is noticed. There is something here, in this young man, that is more than a musician with a harp, or a shepherd with a sling and a crook. *Now* he has Saul's attention.

That is quite a picture! David standing before the king and with a giant's head in his hand and the King asks David in person, "Whose son are you?"

His reply is, "David, son of Jesse".

Now he is known by name.

Now he is identified from the family and household of Jesse.

Now he has the recognition of legitimacy.

Now David is tied to the Royal Court.

Now he has won the hand of the princess – part of the reward bounty for killing the champion, a matter, by the way, that became quite complicated.

Now David is part of the royal army and no longer a shepherd.

This is a victory that makes David, son of Jesse, famous.

It is said that there is a Psalm at is attributed to David that has not made it into our Bible. It is said that David penned this after the battle with Goliath. It is known as Psalm 151, and there were copies of this song found amongst the Dead Sea Scrolls[ii].

Psalm 151

I was small among my brothers,
and the youngest in my father's house;
I tended my father's sheep.
My hands made a harp;
my fingers fashioned a lyre.
And who will tell my Lord?
The Lord Himself; it is He who hears.

It was He who sent His messenger
and took me from my father's sheep,
and anointed me with His anointing oil.
My brothers were handsome and tall,
but the LORD was not pleased with them.

I went out to meet the Philistine,
and he cursed me by his idols.
But I drew his own sword;
I beheaded him,
and took away disgrace from the people of Israel.

A Defeated Foe

David did not go into battle with a sword... but that does not mean he didn't need one. Actually, he really *did* need one. The stone from his sling knocked Goliath out. But it was Goliath's own sword that killed him. David didn't have a sword, yet God provided one. He used the enemy's own weapon against himself. Those things that Goliath declared would cause havoc on God's people were turned around to become the instrument of his undoing and defeat.

What is it like to realise that God can take the weapons of the enemy and turn them around to be a provision in my victory?

Layers of Insight

If we are looking for the prophetic pattern of Messiah in this story, we can identify so many layers in this account:
We can see divine intervention and grace in the life of David.
We see a parallel grace of God's hand on the nation of Israel as his chosen people.

David's boldness was a declaration that regardless of the battle – God is there, willing to empower his people to use the skills that they hold, to defend those he loves... that God is our defender.
God did it for Israel, and he did it for David.

In this account, God took away the disgrace over David, from a nameless shepherd who was treated like a servant... to become recognised as 'David - Son of Jesse'.

We also see that God took away the disgrace over the people of Israel, who were cowering under the threats of an uncircumcised Philistine and the oppression from neighbouring nations.

But there is more. Not only can we see God's overarching story of salvation through the Jews for the Jews, but also the larger story of salvation for humanity. The Battle is not just personal, or local, or even national... but there is a spiritual battle that is also being engaged for humanity. That is the lineage of Messiah.

We are told David took Goliath's head to Jerusalem. There is a very strong school of thought that interprets this to mean, that David buried the head of Goliath on Golgotha[iii]. *That* Golgotha... the place of the skull... the place where Jesus was crucified, was named, not just because it geographically looked like a skull, but it may have also been called... Gol – Gotha... Goliath of Gath... a derivative of merging the two words. David has a prophetic anointing... we see that over and over in his Psalms.

Bible Reading
Psalm 22

Victory Won!

This is of my favourite prophetic psalms. David could see that there is a spiritual battle that is being played out. He wrote about it... he sang about it... and I do wonder, even though it is not explicitly stated in the text... whether David took Goliath's head to Jerusalem and buried it on Golgotha. Was this David's prophetic acknowledgment that there is a bigger war being waged here? That this was not just a battle for the lands and freedom of the Israelites, but also a spiritual battle.

The battle belongs to the Lord! Victory is his! He has done it! The battle that Jesus, the son of God, engaged in... the battle that Jesus fought on the cross, when it stood on a hill called Golgotha, was another David and Goliath moment. Jesus, the Messiah, of the lineage of David, was winning the final and great battle of salvation. That battle Jesus engaged in took the enemy's weapon, the weapon of death, and turned it against Satan, and caused the war to be won!

Final Thoughts...

The story of David and Goliath is one of the most famous stories in the Bible. It is a story of winning against the odds. But it is only that sort of story if we look through the lens of those around us. David did not look through a lens of beating the odds. To David there was no imbalance in power, because he had the God of the Heavens with him, and he carried the name of the LORD.

Every day I meet with people who are confronting Goliaths in their lives. Goliaths that defy the people of God and attempt to intimidate with slander that says we are powerless and have no options available to us. Goliaths that would dare to arrogantly assume that defeat is inevitable. These goliaths may be health related, relationships, financial, or employment issues. David offers a bold example to follow, that we do not face these goliaths with arrogance, or even fear, but with the assurance that God has the last say.

The battle belongs to our God.

The Almighty God of Israel was with David. The scales, in reality, weighed heavily in David's favour. David knew that truth and that is what he listened to. He didn't listen to the fear, nor to the arrogance of the enemy, but to God who was present in his life.

David stands apart, as a young man who carried a warrior's heart. A heart that is bold enough to engage in the fight. Not fearfully, not arrogantly but fully assured that God is fighting with him. God is fighting for him and just like David, it is the health and nature of our heart that determines whether we step into all that God has for us, to win the battles that are in our path.

Prayer:

Father God, thank you that you are the commander of the armies of Heaven. Thank you that your name carries authority. We thank you that you are with us, and we don't have to face giants fearfully. It's not right if we presume to go into battle arrogantly and forgive us when we do. Father, we know we can be fully assured that you've got this. That you are the God who stands by our side, that you are the God that equips our hands and trains us to be fully able to engage the battles that come our way. We ask Father God, that your presence would be with us as we face our Goliaths; that we would not be intimidated by the slanderous accusations that come against us but that we would stand fully assured in the knowledge that you are with us, because you give us the resources that we need. Those resources may even come from

the enemy's hand. We ask your blessing and you protection over us and ask Father God that as we step into this week that we may be people who confidently, assuredly defend the name of Jesus and our God with honour.
We ask this, in Jesus' name, Amen.

3

A Faithful Heart

Where we are...

David, as a young man, lifted disgrace off Israel, when he took up the challenge thrown out by Goliath who stood as the enemy's champion and hero of the Philistines. This event impacted some massive changes in David's life. Some of these were positive and enriching; some of them confusing and challenging. So, let's look at one of the immediate impacts from the victory against the Philistines.

Bible Reading
1 Samuel 18:1-5

Friends for life

David is suddenly thrown into the limelight. He is the hero of Israel! This heroic event catapulted some positive changes. Jonathan is Saul's son. He is a prince in the Kingdom; the royal born heir to Israel's throne. We are told that Jonathan became "one in spirit" with David. He takes pleasure in David's success and his popularity. Jonathan has won his own remarkable victories, yet he does not begrudge David his success. It is said that a true friend, is one who does not just stand by you in tough times but one who can celebrate with you in the good times. There is no envy or bitterness or jealousy because of David's celebrity status and rise to fame. Jonathan loves David "as himself". That is a scriptural turn of phrase.

Bible Reference
Leviticus 19:18

This was the reference point Jesus used when he talked about the gold standard of treating other people well. Treat them with love and the care and kindness, just as you would care for yourself. This is what following Jesus looks like on the ground - this was the friendship these two men shared. Jonathan looked at David through a lens of love, and they became friends for life.

Linked with Covenant

So strong was their friendship that they bound themselves together in a covenant. In other cultures, this might be the binding that might occur as bond-brothers or blood-brothers. Jonathan links his destiny with David, and he confirms this covenant by giving him his princely robe, his tunic, and even his sword, his bow and belt. Did you notice that these were the things that David had plundered from the enemy Goliath? He could take Goliath's things because they were his by right as victor – his reward for winning the conquest. But here Jonathan voluntarily surrenders these same items, not as plunder from a battle, but as solemn gifts sealing their friendship. Jonathan takes those things that would mark himself as a prince – robe, tunic, sword and belt and places them in David's hand, as a sign of his affection and his goodwill and David accepts them as a gesture of this deep and sincere friendship.

Who are the 'strong standing', 'long-standing' friends in my life?

Liked and Successful

David enjoys an extraordinary season of success. He goes from being an unseen attendant – serving in the palace, singing soothing songs when Saul has a bad mood, to being a commander of armies on the battlefield. He climbs through the ranks quickly, from footman to commander and the soldiers in the army are right behind him. He attains experience and victories, and the officers approve. Regardless of what mission King Saul throws David's way he is successful in executing it. These were the positive outcomes from that battle with Goliath but there was also a darker side emerging.

Bible Reading
1 Samuel 18:6-16

A Jealous Rage

Saul had held a level of affection for David. Now this dramatically changes. I find some of the language in this passage difficult to understand. How do we reconcile these passages that say that an "evil spirit from God" came upon Saul? God is completely good and holy.

Bible Reference
James 1:17

God is constant, good, perfect, and yet here, Saul is in a very dark place and the passage attributes that place to God. How do we understand that? We do know a few things that helps with this. We know that Saul has removed himself from God's way. That movement carries consequences. It means he wants to do life independently from God, and God allows it. Saul is now operating without the protection of God. It exposes him to a vulnerability that previously he was protected from. Without the goodness of God in our life, it means we are exposed to experiencing the bad. Saul no longer has the presence of God's Holy Spirit is his life. This means the light has gone out... and it has left a vacuum in his soul. The absence of light is dark. The absence of love is despair. The absence of grace... is jealous rage.

Volatile hate

Where once David's music and songs were soothing... now Saul doesn't hear a soothing ballad but dancing girls singing David's praises. He sees a shepherd boy who gets victory songs sung in his honour and as the nation's sovereign, he does not.

Am I a person who celebrates successes and blessings with other people?

Now Saul notices that David has battle victories, battle scars and is admired by his commanders and his jealousy continues to simmer, and boil, until it explodes.

His rage become volatile, unstable and unpredictable. But in all of this, David eludes the attempts on his life. What a difficult position David is in. He has the love and affection of those in public office. He has the love and affection of the prince. And yet the King himself, the one who used to like him, now seethes at his very name and is trying to kill him.

Over the next passages, Saul makes direct attempts to kill David over and over. Then Saul tries indirect ways to place him in dangerous positions so the enemy would do the dirty work for him. But these plots failed, and David flourishes with even more success.

Victorious reputation!

So, what happened to the promise of being rewarded with the princess's hand in marriage? Remember how King Saul had offered the incentive that whoever killed Goliath would become the King's son-in-law?

Well, it seems that promise went by the way. Until Saul plots to use this as another way to take David out: death by the hand of the enemy. So, he flatters David encourages him to becomes his son in law.

Bible Reading
1 Samuel 18:17-18

The reward had already been promised, yet Saul changes the parameters to include additional requirements. He can have this honour if he will fight on the front line of the fiercest battles against the enemy. David is not afraid of a fight. He fights the battles against the enemies of Israel.

On the promised wedding day Saul marries his oldest daughter off to another man. Notice the moving goal posts – there are shifting agreements, everchanging requirements, unstable promises. This is classic abuse of power. David is now shunned by the King. It doesn't matter what he does, he will not satisfy Saul enough to regain his withdrawn favour.

But David carries on. There is no record of David being offended or incensed. No confrontation or demands are made. Again, Saul is thwarted in his plots against David until he learns that his younger daughter Michal, is already madly infatuated with David. Saul sees another opportunity and encourages his attendants to promote the idea that Michal is really smitten. He offers Michal's hand in marriage to David for the mere bounty of one hundred foreskins of Philistines warriors. Of course, this would demonstrate his courage and worthiness to be the king's son-in-law.

In reality, it is a gruesome and underhanded bride-price, with a time limit and a high danger-quota. Yet David goes over and above: double in fact. He returns with two hundred of the said bride-price bits. How flattering to have David so openly crusade for Michal's hand with double the price! We might smile and admire David's courage, his audacity, and his persistence, but all of this serves to embed Saul's contempt and hatred of David. David has become a double threat. Now he is his son-in-law – a royal member of his household through marriage. His daughter is in love, and he expects she would protect her loved husband rather than betray him in loyalty to her father. Michal does save David's life and provides a decoy so he could escape Saul.

There is a grace-point on David's life in all this drama because he is living in God's light. He is living in the fulness of what Saul had rejected. This is the contrast between light and dark. The darkness of Saul's experience now clashes with David's light. Thus, starts one of the most famous cat and mouse stories in history that lasts for years.

Where have I experienced a vacuum of light?
How did I get there?

Bible Reading
1 Samuel 20:1-42

Parting Ways. Confusion

There is a big question on David's lips: "Why? I don't get it. What have I done?"

In hindsight we can emphatically say 'he did nothing wrong'. This was not about David's failings. David had, in fact, kept his conscience clear. All this opposition was about Saul, and his own personal internal battles. What David was doing was right; and it was his success, that was building resistance and push back from Saul.

Have I ever considered that some problems may come my way... not as consequences of doing something wrong, but as resistance from the dark, because I am living and walking in God's light?

Confirming the facts

David checks in with Jonathan. His friend is perhaps a little naïve assuming that because he loved David, everyone else does too. We see he has no real understanding of the genuine danger David is in, but they work out a plan to confirm the actual lay of the land. There was the test of missing the feast. There is even the incident where Saul has a go at Jonathan and tries to kill him. Now this is real. Jonathan suddenly truly understands that Saul has marked David for death.

Am I a person who stands with others during hard times?

Consolidation of promises

Jonathan devises the code of the arrows, shot into the field. Go further, don't delay! That message means that if David is to live, right now, he lives as a fugitive. David is not coward; he stood up against Goliath... but in this case, he has the wisdom to know which battle to fight and which one to not. Now he is a military man who has gone AWOL.

There is a warrant out for his arrest – dead or alive and his only crime, was being good at what he does, being liked, and excelling.

This picture of Jonathan and David saying goodbye to each other is so moving. Their relationship is torn apart by someone else's bad behaviour and vindictiveness. This is not how it is meant to be. Reconciliation and grace are supposed to be the hallmarks of God's people. Yet, here, we find David is thrown into a place, where everything he had thought marked how he fitted into the scheme of things is no longer available to him. He is on the out. He has lost his place. I am so touched by the grace of Jonathan. He doesn't take on his father's hate; he doesn't abandon his friendship with David. He walks this very fine line between family-loyalty and friendship-loyalty, and I think he does this well. He protects David's life, but doesn't disrespect his father, even though Saul interprets it as such. David and Jonathan renew their covenant of friendship. They confirm their faithfulness to their friendship... regardless of what is happening now and what is going to happen in the future. When life throws us curveballs... we continue on, loving and protecting with a faithful heart.

The experiences of David's life in this part of his story, start out as we expect. David was anointed to be king by Samuel, David on the fast track to the top job. David was popular and respected by his peers. He is the prince's best friend. David wasn't a one-giant-wonder, but he has won battle, after battle, after battle. But now, suddenly all that derails. His quick rise to fame and popularity crashes and burns. David is thrown back into obscurity, hiding for his life.

I remember a particular time when all the things that I thought that I knew about myself, my ministry expression, and the things that God had placed in my hand were suddenly taken away. It left me shellshocked. I had no idea what to do with that. I remember one night, going outside looking at the stars and crying out to God, saying, "I have no idea where I fit anymore. This does not make sense, but I know one thing: I know that you are my faithful God, and you are God that asks questions. Please ask me a question so that I can start to navigate my way through this... because I haven't got a clue. I don't know where I fit anymore."

It was a raw, honest transparent cry, and the question that God dropped into my heart was: 'Where do you know that your already fit?'

I didn't expect that. Now, as I look back over that time, with the scaffolding of counselling that I have studied since, I think, "What a profound question!"

It was exactly what I needed in that moment. I needed to look at some of those things that are constants for me, and to hold on to those: the idea that God was there; God is faithful; it was true that some people had abandoned me, but there were other faithful people who were still in my life.

When things are not what we expect, sometimes it is very hard to hold on to the confidence that God is in this. Just because we can't see how it fits together it doesn't mean God has abandoned us or his promises. David faced the same thing as the opposition from Saul ramps up.

Can I trust that God is consistently good and consistently loving... and he will take those things intended to harm me, and work them for my good?

Bible Reference
1 Samuel 19:18

David had gone to meet with Samuel at Ramah. David was at loss as to what to do and where to go. What now? So, he returns to the man who prophesied destiny over his life. He was consolidating and reminding himself of the promises of God. The circumstances might not look like God is consolidating his own promises to David. But God is...God is not surprised. God is working it all out. God is using what Saul intends for David's undoing, to weave into David's life, strength and character and faithfulness, exactly the kind of fabric a Godly King should have.

How do we know David trusts in God's faithfulness?

We know because we have a Biblical record, and a remarkable anthology of his poetry, songs and psalms that he wrote during this life and Psalm 59 that journalled his relationship with God. Some of these songs were penned after one of Saul's attempts to murder him during this time.

Bible Reading
Psalm 59

David's faithfulness was not just for the brotherhood he shared with Jonathan. First, he was confident in the constant faithfulness of God, who was his fortress, his strength. God is the reliable and faithful one. He wrote about it... he sang about it.

David didn't confuse Saul's bad behaviour with God's unchangeable goodness. God is who keeps him stable when it all seems to be going belly up. This is what kept him firm through uncertain times. It wasn't his popularity with the dancing girls...nor his favour with the king that kept him strong when things were confusing and dark.

What do I need to do, to come back into the light of God's grace and care?

If we are looking for the patterns of Messiah through the prophetic life of David. We can see the echoes of this as he declares the words he wrote in Psalm 59

Bible Reference
Psalm 59:1-4,17

Can I sing of God's strength and love and hide in the fortress of his faithfulness?

We know Jesus was accused without fault or crime. The Messiah was living in God's light.
There is a clash and a confrontation between the light and dark... but the darkness does not overcome it. The light prevails. God prevails.

How would I check that I am faithfully living in the light?

Final Thoughts...

The Apostle John describes Jesus as Messiah like this:

Bible Reference
John 1:3-5

The friendship of David and Jonathan is famous in its loyalty and faithfulness. The jealousy of Saul is equally famous for its malicious intent to destroy him. This meant that the places where David thought he belonged were now ripped away from him. So where did he fit?

That question "Where do you know you already fit?" helped me focus on what I knew when I was navigating a new season... I no longer had a place where I felt comfortable and fulfilled... that had been taken away. I knew I had a husband who loved me... I knew I had a family I trusted... I knew God was my fortress... I knew God is faithful. I once had a picture of a lighthouse that I kept at my workstation... and I had written these words on that picture:
"God is not keeping it from me... he is keeping it for me."
To me that idea was a light, that was an anchor point when things were uncertain. God is Faithful!
When I was back there... as I was trying to work out what life looked like when things had changed so much... I could not have imagined where God would take me, or the richness of the ministry opportunities he would open up for me. I had no concept of where God would position me. But that was what God was keeping for me.

David held onto what he knew... he knew God was his fortress; God had a place where he already fitted. He knew God is faithful. He knew he had a faithful friendship he could trust and from there, even as he was trying to work out what life looked like now, he could not have imagined what God was keeping for him. God was not keeping those promises from him, and as David hung onto those things that he knew, his heart stayed faithful.

David stands apart... as a young man with a faithful heart. His heart is faithful to his friendship with Jonathan, faithfully aligned with God. He recognises God is his fortress, God is his constant... not just in his popularity... not just with his favour with the king or any other influential person. In every aspect of his life, even when it was all falling apart. And just like David, when our confidence is in the constant good nature of God, this is what holds us like a safe fortress, when it seems life is going all wrong. He holds those promises safely for us until the time is right.

Prayer:

Father God, I thank you that you see me in the seasons when it seems that life is perfectly aligned; where things are going well, when people like us and we feel like we are kicking goals.

But Father, I thank you that you also see me when all that changes; when it goes belly up, when there is resistance of darkness against the light of Your presence in my life. We ask Father God that you will help us to be people who stay faithfully aligned with your heart; that we would be the kind of friend who will not only stand beside people in their successes and celebrate that with them but will also stand beside them in their dark times. We ask Father that you will use this story to encourage us and inspire us to build faithfulness into the fabric of our heart. We pray Father that we will not be people who are swayed by unbalanced doctrines or shadows or difficulties, but we will be anchored firmly in your love, with confidence in your faithfulness. Thank you that we can run to you as our fortress.
In Jesus name, Amen.

4

A Refreshed Heart

Where we are...

We are noticing that David didn't arrive to be King on a smooth trajectory of up and forward. In fact, where we left him, he has gone from being the favourite son of Israel, to, now, being a man with a bounty on his head. He has left the palace, his job, his wife, his family... and he is fleeing for his life.

David is now, quite literally, a man on the run, who is living a wilderness experience. As we continue to look at David's story, we are going to consider how we navigate wilderness experiences and keep our hearts soft towards God and be refreshed in the face of hardship.

Seasons in the Wilderness... most people experience them.
I have had a wilderness experience. I remember it as hard and dry and lonely. I also remember God giving me encouragement during that season... promises that it would not always be like this. Every time people prayed for me... the Holy Spirit would give them pictures of gardens, and garlands of flowers for me... even desert flowers... ideas from the story of David as he spent time in the wilderness and was refreshed.
People would give me random gifts... such as mugs with wildflowers on them... and I would be reminded: the wilderness is hard... but it is not forever.

David in the Wilderness

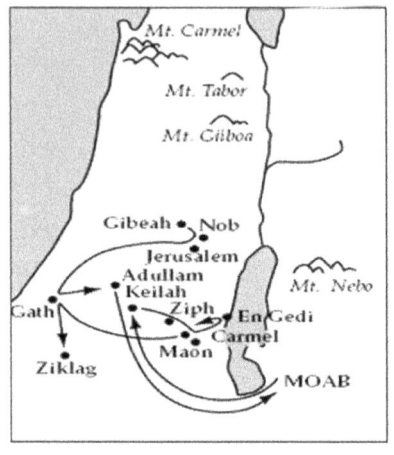

David in the Wilderness
1. Nob – tabernacle
2. Moab
3. Philistine country, Gath – King Achish
4. Cave of Adullam
5. Forest of Hereth
6. City of Keilah – defends it
7. Desert of Ziph
8. Desert of Maon – Carmel
9. En Gedi
10. Crags of the Wild Goats
11. Desert of Paran
12. Desert of Ziph
13. Philistine country – King Achish
14. Philistine country – Ziklag

David's wilderness experience is not a six-week exile... or three months... or even a couple of years. This is an exile that goes on and on. The timeline we are given is not exact, but we have enough information to suggest that the time David was in exile in the wilderness was at least seven years and could have gone on for as long as twelve or more years. We have over fourteen locations documented where he went backwards and forwards from, moving on to the next place to escape King Saul and his army as they chased him down.

That is a long time to keep your head up, and your heart up. But we know that he did keep going, so *how* did David do that? How did he continue to stay strong and not give up during this time? How did he not lose heart when it seems like the promise has gone underground?

Where do I go when I am tired, and thirsty, and need encouragement?

To respond to this idea, we are going to look at three wilderness experiences to see how David accessed encouragement and refreshment when it seems like the promises are a long way away.

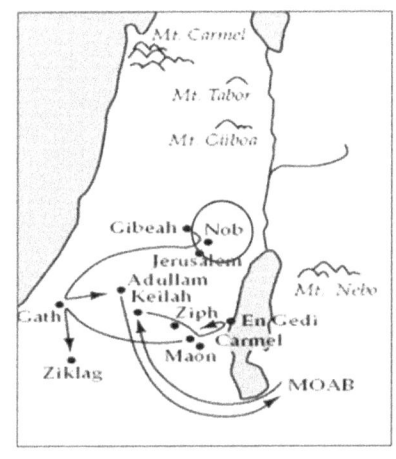

David in the Wilderness
1. Nob – tabernacle
2. Moab
3. Philistine country, Gath – King Achish
4. Cave of Adullam
5. Forest of Hereth
6. City of Keilah - defends it
7. Desert of Ziph
8. Desert of Maon - Carmel
9. En Gedi
10. Crags of the Wild Goats
11. Desert of Paran
12. Desert of Ziph
13. Philistine country – King Achish
14. Philistine country – Ziklag

David in the Wilderness: The Tabernacle at Nob

The first account we will look at is right at the beginning as David flees for his life and he goes to the Ahimelek the Priest at the tabernacle at Nob.

Bible Reading
1 Samuel 21:1-10

Suddenly David is on the run. He has escaped without food or weapon and the place he goes to is the house of the Lord, The Tabernacle. Nob is a community outside of Jerusalem where the tabernacle of God was during this time. Nob was known as a community of priests. David goes there, perhaps for rations, perhaps for encouragement and sustenance that is more than just physical. It has been a long-standing controversy that David, lies about his circumstances, and then ate the consecrated Shew Bread from the tabernacle to survive.

Where has God provided bread and strength for me in unexpected places?

Jesus references this account in Matthew chapter 12:

Bible Reference
Matthew 12:1-8

Jesus uses this story to reassure those who would try to screw down on the letter of the law by showing that David was not condemned by God in these circumstances. Jesus even said that the law is not there to judge us, but there to guide us. Rather God is a God who refreshes us when we come to him in our dry times and in our desperate times.

David also asks the priest Ahimelek for a weapon. But this is a place of worship, not an armoury. The priest tells David that there is no weapon, except the sword of Goliath. The sword of the enemy... something that David had given over to God and dedicated to him. I wonder what it was like for David to unwrap it and hold it in his hand. Can you imagine him weighting it in his grip once more?

What an incredible reminder! God had provided a sword for him in the past. God had given him everything he needed in a moment of great confrontation. That same God would again make what he needed available to him in this moment. God had provided for him again, not just his practical needs, but the spiritual, mental, emotional encouragement that he went looking for.

Can I look back and take hold of a token of a past victory in my hand, to encourage me in what I am dealing with now?

A Song of hope

Ahimelek the priest was very unsettled when David turns up alone. And rightly so, for Doeg, the king's shepherd saw David at the Tabernacle. He later reports to the king that David had gone there, and Saul orders the massacre of Ahimelek and 85 priests from Nob. When Saul's guards refused to raise a hand against the priests, he has Doeg execute this atrocity. Doeg was a shepherd, who had an axe to grind against the rise of David – who had also been a shepherd. Doeg would do even this to buy favour with King Saul.

It is a difficult thing to acknowledge that your presence – even in a moment of desperation, has caused the death of 86 innocent men of God. David wrote Psalm 52 after he received the news that the priests of Nob had all been massacred because of their contact with David. It gives us some idea how David restores and recovers and encourages himself in the face of horrifying and very distressing circumstances.

Bible Reading
Psalm 52

David brings himself back to the hope that he has, in God, when the world around him is going crazy. He sings of his hope in the presence of the Lord. His hope is in his God of faithfulness, of unfailing love. His hope is in God's name, because it is a good name. His hope is like an olive tree, flourishing, deeply rooted, sourcing its nourishment in the word and worship of God. The next account is when David is hiding in the caves of Adullam:

Bible Reading
1 Samuel 22:1-4

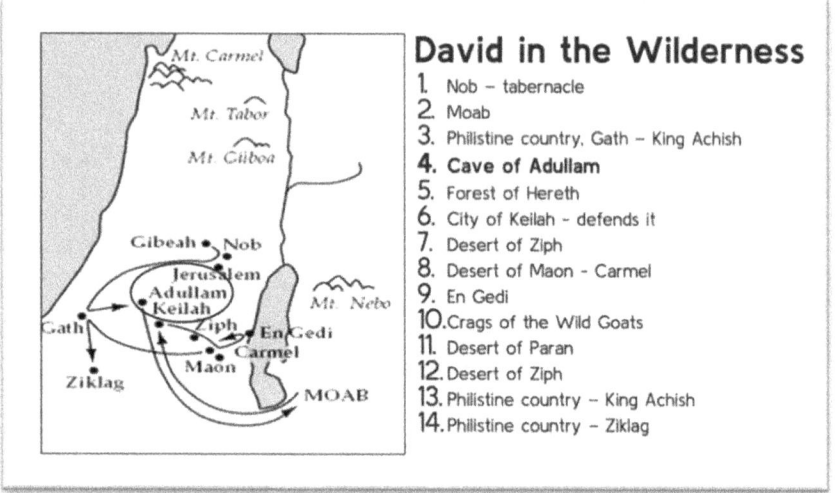

David in the Wilderness – Cave of Adullam

The Cave of Adullam was also known as 'The Stronghold'. It is also a word that means a 'Hiding Place' or 'Refuge'. There was a spring nearby, so there was provision of water there. This network of caves was large enough to accommodate 400 men, and it is here, in exile, that David attracts all sorts of people to his side who are also seeking refuge. We also see that David's brothers join him – even Eliab, who previously called David a 'wicked' upstart who was just out for an entertaining view of the battle with Goliath. There was a gathering of all types, but particularly those who were distressed, in debt or discontented.

Have I come from a place of distress, debt or discontent?

What a way to build an army. What a way to build a church! This is disfunction 1-0-1. All sorts of displaced people go to David and find a place of belonging. Here, they found a sense of refuge from what was troubling them. Most likely they also brought their discontent, their distress, and the issues that had found them in debt, with them. Yet David welcomes them in. He builds cohesion and works to give them purpose and an identity that was missing before.

David becomes their 'commander'. I notice the language.
Not king – they are not his subjects.
Not CEO – they are not his workforce.
Not leader – they are not his minions.
Not pastor – they are not his parishioners.
A Commander.

David is building an 'army' under a military model. That is what he knew. He is starting with what he knew, what he had, and was building something more, something better, something exceptional.

When David first heard Goliath's intimidating taunts at the front line, there was not one man in all of Israel who would stand up valiantly and fight for what is right. But when we fast forward, to years down the track, when David is King, when he is back in the Caves of Adullam, fighting the enemy, tired and thirsty, and discouraged, we see something quite different.

We see mention made of the fact that after David is King, he had thirty chief warriors, who were known as 'David's Mighty Men'. This list of 'Mighty Men' was the Honours List of exceptional capable and courageous fighters. These were the elite Special Forces: remarkable, brave, bold, outstanding, noteworthy, honoured. Where once, that sort of courage was only found in one young shepherd in all of Israel, by the time David is King, that sort of outstanding courage becomes a new normal.

What is it like to remind myself that God is moving me towards being distinguished and valiant and courageous?

Bible Reference
2 Samuel 23:13-17

King David is in the Caves of Adullam, regrouping from battle. Three of David's Mighty Men heard David wistfully desire a drink from the well at Bethlehem, his hometown. At that time, it was being held by the Philistines. It was not that David was literally thirsty, because there was water at the caves of Adullam. David just wanted that water from home, a longing perhaps of a simpler time.

These three mighty men, break through the enemy lines and literally bring King David back some water from the well at Bethlehem. It seems they have no other agenda, other than to serve their king, their commander, and to refresh his soul. That is loyalty. They had done the impossible. They had done it at the risk of their lives. That is dedication!

Where have I considered that the effort and the investment of my service hardly seems worth it?

When King David realised what they did, he refused to drink the water they brought back. That's confusing. They went to all this effort and now he just pours it out on the ground?

Dedicated Offering

But let's pause. Remember this was during the era of Tabernacle worship. There were specific sacrifices that were understood and accepted forms of worship. One of these sacrifices was called a "Drink offering". Paul, at the end of his life, talked about being "poured out like a drink offering". This 'drink offering' was a sacrificial offering – sacred to God. It was an offering of joy, of completion, of fulfilment.

This water from Bethlehem was not undiluted wine as required for this drink offering, but the sacrifice made by the men, so they could bring it to David, made it just as potent. King David said that it represented the blood of the men who went to get it for him. David is acknowledging the sacrifice, the effort, the investment, the intention, the courage. *That was a sacrifice* before the Lord - *that* is what completes it. The water itself is less refreshing than the investment behind that act.

What is it like to think of your perseverance and investment as a drink offering?

When this happened, King David was in a cave, using it as a safe place to regroup and refresh. His men's courage and generosity truly refreshed him.

But let's go back to where we are in David's story as he is running from Saul. He is not yet King, and these caves becomes a place where the people who gather around him are described as distressed and indebted and discontented. Yet David sees something quite different. David is working with what other people had discarded, and he sees in these men, an army of valiant, mighty warriors. He could see qualities in these discontents, and he was moving, and shifting them towards a place of honour. Every time he needed refreshment, there was a source of water in the desert places that was not just about the springs of Adullam, or the well at Bethlehem, but an offering of sacrifice poured out before God, a place of refreshment and restoration.

David had an awareness, regardless of whether this worked out in the end or not, that God saw and honoured the effort, the investment, a sacrifice, the worship, right now. And that was an acceptable offering to God. David knew God sees this heart... the investment part... the hard part... the persevering part... and that is enough. There are a couple of Psalms that David wrote while he was in the cave.

Bible Readings
Psalm 142:1-3
Psalm 57:1-3 &9-10

How remarkable to read these Psalms, keeping in mind the setting in which they were written. Refreshment in the desert: "I will Awaken! I will Sing! I will Praise! I *will* intentionally dedicate this offering as a sacrifice of praise."

Can I trust that God is my stronghold, my fortress, my safe place?

Can I sing of God's unfailing love... and source of refreshment?

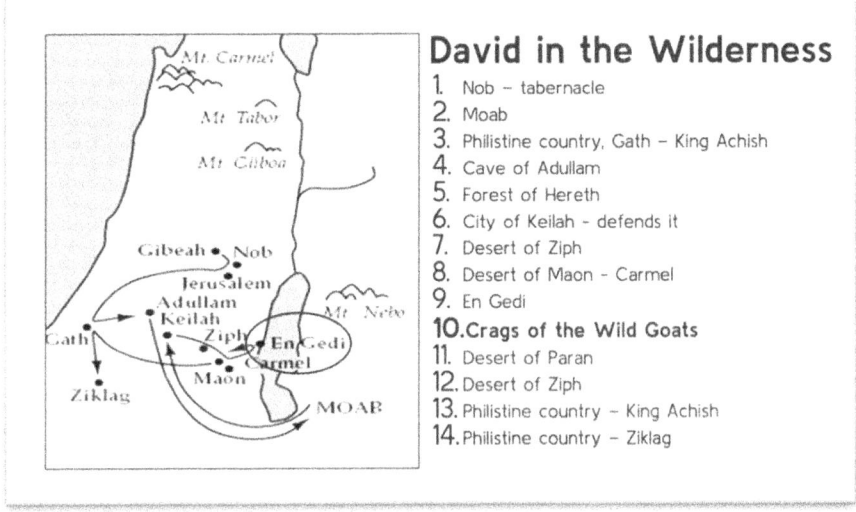

David in the Wilderness
1. Nob – tabernacle
2. Moab
3. Philistine country, Gath – King Achish
4. Cave of Adullam
5. Forest of Hereth
6. City of Keilah – defends it
7. Desert of Ziph
8. Desert of Maon – Carmel
9. En Gedi
10. Crags of the Wild Goats
11. Desert of Paran
12. Desert of Ziph
13. Philistine country – King Achish
14. Philistine country – Ziklag

David in the Wilderness – Crags of the Wild Goats

During this wilderness period, we come to another account that occurs at a place identified as the Crags of the Wild Goats, which is probably in the En Gedi.

Bible Reading
1 Samuel 24:2-13

This region is a barren, rocky, hard place but it also is a place that has natural springs hidden in the rocks, suitable for shepherds to tend their flocks and that area also had a system of natural caves to hide in.

There are many accounts in the Bible that are honest and unglamorous. Can you imagine seeing the king going to the toilet right in front of you, bare butt and all... without paper!

David's men declare, "This is the hand of God!" They saw this as a Divine opportunity! There were 3000 strong young soldiers in the King's regiment searching for David, against, possibly 400 discontents from David's band. They declare that God has to be in this! They even say, "This is God's promise to you!"

But it should be truthfully noted that God never promised to deliver *'Saul into David's hands for him to deal with him as he wished.'* That was just the men talking. They were spiritualising an event, when it wasn't like that at all. We know this because of the way David handled it. It was a bit cheeky – cutting of a piece of Saul's robe but as soon as David did that, the Holy Spirit convicted him. God was positioning David, not to overthrow Saul by his own sword, not to handle it his own way. It was not David's role to take matters into his own hand.
So yes, it was an opportunity, but not the one that his men were suggesting.

How do I respond when those against me are right in front of me in a vulnerable place?

This was an opportunity to stand strong to his convictions, and to choose to handle this honourably. *'From evildoers come evil deeds.'*

David does not spiritualise something evil and call it the hand of God. This was an opportunity for David to hold fast to the understanding that he was not responsible for Saul's choices, but he *was* responsible for his own. This was an opportunity to continue on, *and* continue on, *and* continue on, *and* to persevere through the wilderness. An opportunity to step back into a position of trust knowing that God is his stronghold, God is his refuge, God is his strength.

Would I see this as an opportunity for revenge or better positioning, or trusting God?

Bible Reading
Psalm 27

David makes a renewed commitment to do things God's way... not his own way. It is a commitment to keep going even when, where he is right now, it is dry and unfair and discouraging.

Can I step back into a position of trust and renew my commitment to doing things God's way?

Even when those around you are saying this is a God opportunity. And it might be... but not in the way they are suggesting. David has the wisdom to discern the difference. David is in a place of waiting, in a wilderness place, and he took heart and stayed strong.

Final Thoughts...

For years David was pursued by King Saul and his men, in an unrelenting manhunt. He was literally living in a wilderness, a dry and thirsty place and yet he did not lose hope, or courage, or strength. He goes to God for sustenance and holds a reminder of God's provision from a previous battle, in his hand. He sees the potential of what other people discarded and dedicates all of his effort and investment as an offering before God, even if he would never taste the end result. He sees every situation as an opportunity to do the right thing, not as a short cut to where God has promised to position him.

This is a painting of contrasts: the barren, the hard, the discouragement... and then there is also a place of refreshment, tall trees and clear water, fruitfulness and abundance.
I sketched this picture during that same wilderness time I shared earlier. There was a lot of barrenness in my life and not much experience of

refreshment. But I drew this as a declaration of trust – a declaration that God is present, even in the wilderness times. David wrote songs, this picture was my way of confirming my belief that God was moving me into a place that would be refreshing and fruitful and abundant.

The idea, as I laid it down in my sketch book, didn't look at all like this painting but I appreciated the idea behind it. I remember saying to God as I looked at it afterwards, "I would really like to put this onto canvas at some point... so that I remember what this was like, and what you are going to do..."

One day, we were visiting family, and we bumped into their neighbours. We had known them from a church we had attended, and I just asked, quite generally, how she was going. She said she was enjoying her painting. I hadn't even remembered she was a visual arts lecturer. So, I asked if I could bring our daughter over so we could do some art together. She was home schooled, and I simply thought it was a fun idea that we could paint and have a grown-up playdate together.

When we arrived at her home, this lady had easels and canvases laid out. Then she asked, "What do you want to paint?" I had no idea. I flicked through my sketch pad and found my rather crude sketch. I had forgotten about it. In an afternoon, in some way, she drew this picture out of me. That is a testimony to her skill as a teacher and an artist. Perhaps it was also an answer to a prayer, so that I would not forget. Perhaps in a way, this was my Psalm...

I have engraved a plague on the frame that says:
> "This land that was laid waste
> has become like the garden of Eden'..."
> (Ezekiel 36:35)

Regardless of how it ends up... how can I remind myself that God is faithful?

David stands apart as a man who turns to God to refresh his heart. He recognises God is his stronghold, God is his source, not those around him. Just like David, our refreshment comes from God first. It is he who holds us and refreshes us when life is hard and dry like a wilderness.

Prayer:

Father God, I thank you that you are my stronghold... you are my refuge. Thank you that I can go to you to refresh my soul knowing that in you I can gather strength and encouragement. I thank you, Father that even in the wilderness times you do not leave me, but you hold me and draw me forward into the things that you are keeping for me. I ask Father God that I would be a person who is mindful of others and their personal wilderness experiences.

Father, I also want to be a person of encouragement. Build in me that sort of courage that would break through enemy lines to bring a fresh cup of water to someone who is in need. We thank you for these stories and pray that I can carry some of the truth that they share into our week as I interact with my family, my workplace, and my friends.
In Jesus name, Amen.

5

An Offended Heart

Where we are...

While David was in exile in the wilderness, we have many stories documented where he keeps moving on to the next place to escape King Saul and his army as they chased him down. Unlike the other accounts, this is a story where David does not do so well.

David is human, and just because he is identified as a man after "God's own heart" there is a tendency for us to consider that he always got it right, that he always made the better choice, that he always turned to God, rather than his own flawed emotions and pain.

For our fourth wedding anniversary we went out for lunch and then afterwards, we were at a loose end, so we decided to go see a romantic movie together. We looked at the board outside the cinema and chose a movie based on the actors and there was the word "comedy" included in the brief somewhere.

The movie was called the "War of the Roses" and it was the worst possible movie for a wedding anniversary! But other anniversaries have come and gone, and I still remember that particular date.

When they called this a comedy, if I had read the reviews properly, they were referring to "black, acid-tipped" comedy and I didn't find it funny. Horror movie was more accurate.

It was the most escalated war between a couple: Mr and Mrs Rose, of what happens when offense is not dealt with well.

Over and over there was this hope in me, wanting to believe that an amicable resolution could be achieved but it just kept going, and going, and going.

There was no happy ending. Thank you, Danny DeVito, who directed it. What is more horrifying, is that the movie is based on a real couple, Michael and Rona Rose, who lived in Miami.

I think the take-aways from that particular anniversary date was that I needed to screen the choice of movie beforehand a little more thoroughly and handle offense quickly and well.

As we continue looking at story of David, we are going to consider a time when David doesn't handle offense so well. Fortunately for us, the Bible does not white-wash David's humanness, and we have some accounts where he makes some poor choices that are not honourable. This story occurs right smack-bang in the middle of his wilderness season. David now has around him 600+ men who have come to him distressed, in debt and discontent, and David has the job of giving them purpose and industry in a barren place. That is no small ask.

One way he would do that is to raid Israel's enemies – the outlying communities of the Philistines, and raze their villages to the ground, so that there were no witnesses that could report back that it was David who led these attacks. Remember. David is a soldier. He is not an accountant. He is anointed and called as a warrior in the Kingdom of Israel. He is at war against the enemies of Israel, whether the reigning King of Israel recognises him or not. So, David continues to engage in that calling, by using the opportunities that he has, until God moves him to the next place, or next position.

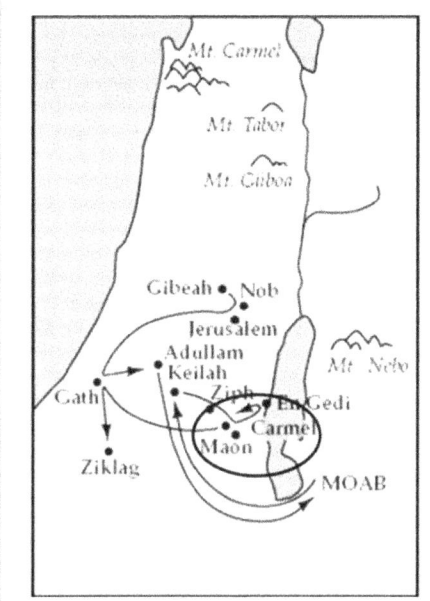

David in the Wilderness

1. Nob – Tabernacle
2. Philistine country, Gath
3. Cave of Adullam
4. Moab
5. Forest of Hereth
6. City of Keilah - defends it
7. Desert of Ziph
8. **Desert of Maon - Carmel**
9. En Gedi
10. Crags of the Wild Goats
11. Desert of Paran
12. Desert of Ziph
13. Philistine country – King Achish
14. Philistine country – Ziklag

David in the Wilderness – Desert of Maon

Another way David builds capacity in this band of rag-tag soldiers was to mobilise them to protect against foreign raiders who would come in and attack the people living in Israel. This is what we find David doing in Chapter 25:

Bible Reading
1 Samuel 25:1-9

Life constantly offers change. Samuel died. Samuel had been a constant in Israel for a long, long time and now that era closes. Samuel never got to see David sit on the throne outside his prophetic vision and faith. He went to his death, believing the promise that God would position a good man on the throne of Israel. There was a period of national mourning for a giant in the faith, then almost immediately,

David moves. He goes to the Desert of Paran near Moan, and I wonder, if there was an unsettling, a grief that David was experiencing from the death of Samuel, that caused him to tilt off his normally very stable axis. It *is* in times of stress, grief and loss where we can be vulnerable to not handle situations as well as we might normally do.

So, it is here in the Desert of Moan, that they have another opportunity to find occupation for his men. David tasks his men with not just being a group of bandits raiding the enemies, but protectors of the citizens of Israel. Bandits and Raiders from the surrounding tribal groups would regularly swoop in. It had been this way for generations. Here, in this area, David's military presence causes the sheep-duffing to stop. He protects the locals – serving their wellbeing. The raiders now have a wall of protection around the local farms that they have to penetrate first.

I read one opinion that described David was running some sort of corrupt regional Protection Racket, unbidden and unwanted, demanding payment on the threat of the locals' livelihoods and their lives. But I don't read this story like that.

If you have 600 men who have a background in their recent histories of being discontent and renegade, they need a purpose. They need work. If you are trying to move them from a place of discontent to a positive place, they need purposeful occupation. One of these local land-barons was a well-establish man named Nabel near the area of Carmel (which is different to Mt Carmel featured in the story of Elijah). Nabel was rich and influential man, but unfortunately, he is also described as boorish, surly and mean. He was not nominated for Employer of the Year. Yet David and his men never stole from him. They protected his men and stock, and then they waited for the accepted time for recognition of their services.

The end of the Shearing season was celebrated as the 'harvest festival' of the pastoralist. During the history of the Australian wool boom, after the last of the woolclip was taken in, the bigger stations would host a lavish Shearing carnival. The bigger the place – the bigger the celebration. Jondaryan, on the Darling Downs, was a huge sheep station during 1860s, and their post shearing festival featured horseracing, footraces, novelty events and competitions that culminated in a lavish feast and a Ball.

Nabel's celebration was this kind of event. It was extravagant display of this man's wealth and prosperity. Nabel was splashing his money around for the community to see. During this event, David respectfully sends a delegation to have some supplies provided to his men, in recognition for their services. Let's see how that went:

Bible Reading
1 Samuel 25:10-17

Nabal is obviously not an idiot. He hasn't lived with his head under a rock. Nabal knew exactly who David was; he knew David was the son of Jesse and he knew David was running from Saul. He dismisses David out of hand. He takes the benefits, without any sense of obligation or honour. Nabal is a taker.

It is not surprising that David is offended. Massively offended. This was disgusting treatment and David's anger escalates to rage. He goes from zero to a hundred in a moment. I hold to the school of thought that tells us our emotions are not wrong or right in themselves. Even the ugly and uncomfortable emotions. Even the difficult emotions of anger, rage and disgust. The emotion themselves is an internal messenger that can inform us of our situation. Our emotions are provided by God in his design of human psyche to tell us something about our situation.

When we learn to read and regulate our emotions well, they can help us better understand what is going on. Our responsibility is to slow down and choose honourable and appropriate responses to our situation.

The intensity of David's anger is a message telling him that this situation is wrong. It is insulting, it is demeaning, it is unjust, and it is grossly unfair. Yep – I get that.

But David doesn't do what he has done in the past. Normally he takes a pause, normally he reflects and prays and considers his options, and chooses a response that will serve him, his men and his God in the best way. But this time, rather than doing that, he straight away calls him men to arms, and activates an attack against Nabal. He is offended and is out for revenge.

Have I ever held offense in my heart so strong that I couldn't think of anything but revenge?

What could I do to slow this process down?

For this Commander, it means razing the community Nabel has built around himself to the ground and obliterating the lot. If Nabel wouldn't offer a gift of acknowledgement, then David was going to take it as loot, an act of warfare, with a lot a suffering thrown into the mix for good measure.

This is a rash response. It is violent and impulsive. But there is a servant in Nabal's household that reads all the signs. He sees disaster hanging over the wild festivities, and over his master's household. This man is obviously not drinking in the thick of the party with the others; he is clear-headed and concerned, and he activates a more considered response. This servant goes to Abigail – Nabal's wife. Abigail is described as beautiful and intelligent, and I would add, sensible and astute.

How can I develop my own ability to be able to support others by being astute and considered?

When the servant tells Abigail what is going on she activates a response to this news.

Bible Reading
1 Samuel 25:18-36

Abigail loads up a supply train of donkeys and sends it on ahead of her. There is nothing to suggest that she thinks what David was asking for, was misplaced or outside any locally understood protocol. She intercepts and cuts across his plan for destruction. They said it was done quickly but we are not talking about throwing together a couple of loaves of day-old bread, and few cans of coke into a basket. These were rations to supply an army – enough for 600 men. This was attending to what had been dismissed out of hand by her husband.

She bows to David in a sign of respect as a dignitary, not a bushranger. I notice that Abigail does not whitewash the reality of her husband's behaviour. She openly acknowledges that Nabal has behaved badly.

She calls him by name: Nabal means "Fool". This type of foolishness is not about being ridiculous, but *'Belial' - without profit, worthless*; evil; ungodly; wicked. This type of *'folly'* is vile villainy. This is damning assessment of a person's character. But the point of Abigail's message, was not how hopeless her husband is, but she is saying, *'David, you are not like this!'* She obviously knows David by reputation as well.

Remember that David, a few years ago, was the talk of every living room and every dining table. Abigail refers to the battles David has won. She refers to his upright and honourable reputation, she even alludes to his victory over Goliath: *"the lives of your enemies he will hurl away as from the pocket of a sling."* She even discloses that she knows that he is anointed to rule over Israel as King, the Lord's promise to build a lasting dynasty. She intercepts his current plan for destruction with a reminder of who he is and what he has been called to. By doing this, she intercedes for her household and the lives of her husband's men.

What I really appreciate in this exchange, is that Abigail encourages David to take the pause that he was unable or unwilling to put in place himself in the first instance.

Who are the people I could check in with, when I am being impulsive?

She acknowledged that what went down was wrong and unfair. She causes David to consider an honourable response to this unjust and unfair situation. Abigail tells David that what he is intending to do as he is headed to war against the house of Nabal... is not just against Nabel, but against his own destiny. If David continues down *this* track, he is going to undo every good choice, every wise decision, every discerning response he has made to this point. Eventually, that could mean David ends up in a place that looks very much like Nabal or King Saul. They might have position, wealth and influence but they do not have the good character to go with it.

Do you notice, that in all the times when David has fought battles previously, he never lifted a hand against the people of Israel? Here, he was making the very people whom God had anointed him to protect, into the enemy. That was his mandate, regardless of whether they are easy or difficult people to get along with. What he was about to do would be remembered not as a victory but as a ruthless and ungodly bloodbath.

Nabal was known as a taker, but here David was choosing to do exactly the same. He was setting himself up as king and judge when he has not been given that authority yet. David was tempted to take the short-cut, and avenge his hurt pride, and his offended feelings. *That* is not the way of God.

David's wisdom is that he does listen to Abigail, and he acknowledges that behind this pretty messenger, was also the hand of the Lord God – Jehovah Elohim. The self-existent, the eternal, the supreme judge. Ultimately David is responsible to God as his judge and is answerable and accountable to God first. It was not right for David to avenge his offense in this way. He acknowledges his intent, and thanks Abigail for her astute thinking.

Do I listen to the Abigails in my life?

What gets in the way of me being able to consider what they say?

This is not the end of the story of Abigail. She makes an appeal to David. This was a declaration of her belief in God's plan and destiny over David. She asks to be remembered when he rises to that place of influence. This is how that petition was fulfilled by David.

Bible Reading
1 Samuel 25: 31, 37-42

This is a story of being seen and remembered. God saw Abigail's life – living in an abusive relationship... and how she consistently held herself above the gross behaviour of her husband. God saw Nabal's harsh disregard and bigoted treatment of his chosen king elect. He has a stroke and dies. The consequences of our life-style choices can be used by God. This reminded David that God had not forgotten him, even in the wilderness.

The message that Abigail boldly carried to David, along with the lamb chops, the wine and the dates... was this: "You *are* anointed King, but you are not there *yet* but how you carry yourself *in the meantime*, will also determine your destiny. That is *your* responsibility. The *timing* of that destiny is God's responsibility!" David had made an oath to Abigail, and as soon as he hears of Nabal's fate he makes good on that oath and marries her as a widow, and she becomes his responsibility.

You may notice I love reading various traditions around these scriptural stories, particularly from various Hebrew rabbinical traditions. There is a story, that when Abigail gets down off the donkey, she shows a bit of thigh, and David burns with passion[iv]. There was chemistry between these two. Part of that tradition was acknowledging that the situation was not just about avenging Nabal's offense to his men, but also about his desire to rescue Abigail from an unscrupulous cur. That way he could take Abigail as his wife straight away. But Abigail reminds David that this is also a matter of timing; she is married and not available. David chooses not to take the path of a taker. He was not going to take what is not *his* to take. He chooses the higher route, as an honourable man of God... and trains himself in the ways of honourable King even before he has arrived in that position.

Is there someone in my life that I can see who is jeopardising their best potential and God given call?

How can I support them to get back on track?

In this story, in just 10 days, that all changes, and David invites Abigail to become his wife. I love Abigail's response to this proposal "I am your handmaiden". She was also not going to be a taker. She was not positioning herself as a future queen of Israel but came with the intent to serve, to wash feet... even the feet of David's men... the unruly and discontents that gathered around him in the wilderness.

Am I a person who is after royal positioning or an opportunity to wash feet?

There are shadows of the example of Jesus coming through David's story again, but this time – not from David.
Abigail intercedes for mercy.
Abigail saves her husband's household from destruction.
Abigail gently but firmly restores and directs David back to his true path.
Abigail doesn't self-promote; but humbly serves, even washing feet.

So, Abigail leaves the lifestyle of an influential first wife of a land baron to join a bushranger with a bounty on his head, who is living in caves out in the wilderness. That is a big change to make but I love the idea that Abigail is joining David in this in-between place, in the meantime. She is fully confident that all these promises will be fulfilled. That is such a declaration of faith. Faith that God remembers his promises, that God is faithful, that God was opening an opportunity for her to be part of the royal household, that God remembers and restores.

Final Thoughts...

For years, David was living in the wilderness with the responsibility of being the commander of over 600 men. Part of this means that he needs to find them appropriate occupation. When he is in the Desert of Moan, he takes the opportunity to protect the locals from foreign raiders. But when David is taken advantage of and insulted, he is offended, and he goes in for revenge.

I remember that challenging family season of trying to manage young toddlers in church. This particular day, our youngest daughter had a 'moment'. Children do have moments. It is a developmental reality. As parents, we had decided to take an approach of "intentional ignoring". It is a recognised strategy, but in hindsight, probably not a suitable one for implementing in church. I came from a background where ministers would say, "Nah, don't worry about it, I can talk louder than your child", and they would just wind up the volume.

But this particular day, the Pastor stopped. He stared at my screaming child and told the lady sitting beside me to take her disruptive child outside. I was mortified. I bundled my daughter and my humiliation up and went out.

What a terrible moment! I was so embarrassed. Every face turned and gave me a very judgemental "evil eye". I was horrified by my inability to read the situation. After all, I had grown up in churches! But children will sometimes surprise us with their resilience and ability to throw a quality tantrum, even in inconvenient places. So, I wrote a letter to the pastor apologising for that miscalculation. That to me, was the end of it.

I was surprised by what happened next. When the pastor got my card, he rang me up. He got his secretary to send me a card and the gist of it was this: he was very grateful that I wasn't offended by what happened and wanted to express his appreciation that I handled it is this way. He told me people have left churches over this sort of situation.

The truth is, I was offended. Very much so. The situation was embarrassing and horrible. I was put under the spotlight as a parent and came up short. That was the message of the emotion of embarrassment. But feeling embarrassed and offended does not dictate my response. It doesn't mean I have to be spiteful back. As I paused, and prayed, I felt God was inviting me to choose to respond in a way that diffused the situation, rather than causing more pain and alienation.

Abigail steps forward to intercept an offended David. She was able to intercede and redirect him to a different path. She acknowledges what happened was offensive, she validates the wrong and she appeals to David to be the better person anyway. This is what David needed. He needed someone to appeal to his better judgement, to take pause and to choose an honourable way of dealing with the awful experiences he encountered in that season of waiting for his promises to be fulfilled.

If I am in an in-between place, am I a person who is able to carry myself responsibly and honourably in the meantime?

Prayer:

Father God, we thank you that in your wisdom you have made us as human. You have given us emotions. That also means you have also given us the experiences of anger, disgust and embarrassment. We pray that you will help us; to take pause and to notice what these messages are telling us. Father, we ask that you would help us not act on reflex – not to strap on a sword and fight for blood, but to take a more responsible and considered response. Holy Spirit, give us wisdom and courage to choose the way we speak, to choose the way we act, so that it is honouring to you, honouring to Jesus. Father God, help us not to sabotage the plans and the purposes you have for us by recklessness. May we be able to step more fully into what you have created us to be, step into more fully to what you have called us to do.
We ask these things in the beautiful and precious name of Jesus. Amen.

6

A Wounded Heart

Where we are...

David has been in exile in the wilderness for many years. He has a company of people around that is now a small army. They move from place to place to stay ahead of King Saul's army that is pursuing him.

David in the Wilderness – Philistine country - Ziklag

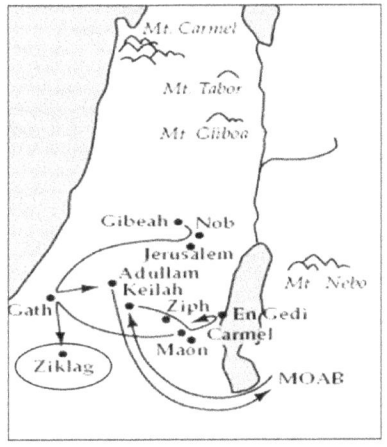

David in the Wilderness
1. Nob – tabernacle
2. Moab
3. Philistine country, Gath – King Achish
4. Cave of Adullam
5. Forest of Hereth
6. City of Keilah - defends it
7. Desert of Ziph
8. Desert of Maon - Carmel
9. En Gedi
10. Crags of the Wild Goats
11. Desert of Paran
12. Desert of Ziph
13. **Philistine country – King Achish**
14. **Philistine country – Ziklag**

I had a conversation with a friend who had a car accident while they were on holidays. The car had flipped a number of times down the highway and was written off. No one was at fault. No one was hurt. I remember talking with him afterwards, and he said as he was standing in the road looking at this mangled mess when they were supposed to be having a restful holiday, and he said to God, "Why is this happening?"

And when he said that my heart stopped. I have long understood that sometimes "why questions" spiral and don't go anywhere. But what he told me made an impact. "No... this was more along the lines that I really wanted to understand what God was teaching me through this. I wanted to understand 'the lesson'," he said.

He said that the Holy Spirit spoke to him, "Life happens and this is my protection..."

Sometimes life throws some terrible wounds at us and now we are looking at some of wounds David experienced while he was in hiding. This next story occurs when he is so alienation in his own land that that he flees to live in Philistine territory.

Bible Reading
1 Samuel 27:1-7

Living in Exile: Alienated & Displaced

How hard it must have been for David to leave Israel to find refuge amongst those "Uncircumcised Philistines" – the people of Goliath. This is a difficult place he finds himself... where the enemies he has fought, are safer than his own people. Yet this is where David has ended up. Alienated and pursued; displaced living in exile, in enemy territory.

Yet what I notice is that David doesn't hide like mistletoe in these Philistine branches, latching on to survive. He has a strong sense of protocol. He goes to the top... he goes to the King. It is not explicitly stated... but it is assumed that King Achish was not the same king who was ruling Israel during the battle of Goliath. It seems Achish is young and finding his feet, dependent on the counsel of those around him. But he likes David, even though they had met before. David had gone to

King Achish before to seek refuge when he first was fleeing from King Saul but when David realised the army officials recognised him as the one that song was written about: *"Saul has slain his thousands; David has slain his tens-of-thousands!"* David feared for his life. So, that time David pretended to be a crazy lunatic frothing and drooling, at the mouth making senseless marks on the walls and gates.

Achish looked at David behaving like a madman and said, "I've got enough crazies of my own, I don't need to import one. Get rid of him. Send him away!"

But this time David finds favour in the court of King Achish as a sane person, as someone who had valuable skills as a contributing soldier with battle experience.

Assigned Ziglag

David's little band of discontent men is growing rapidly as more and more of Saul's men defect over to David. David requests a base to live in. King Achish honours that request and assigns David the town of Ziglag. The families move in; they start to settle down and send down roots. Finally, they have a home. The refugee days are over. They have a place to call home that isn't a cave, or canvas under the stars. The women are more content, the kids are happy. Things are looking up. Life develops a more settled rhythm. Until… it doesn't.

It is important to remember that Ziglag was never the plan: it was a transition place. We cannot confuse transition places with the final destination. We know that this time in Israel's history was dominated by a culture of war. So soon Israel and the Philistines are back at it, but this time David is on the other side of the border. Now he is facing war against his own people.

Have I confused transition places with the final plan?

Bible Reading
1 Samuel 29:1-7

Rejection – from his King

David is living in exile; King Saul doesn't want him anything but for David to be dead. Saul has been reigning over Israel for 40 years at this point, but his mission against David has not abated.

Rejection – from the enemy

The enemy doesn't want David either. King Achish is a converted David believer but that does not extend to those under him. David is excluded again. But wait… there is more.

Bible Reading
1 Samuel 30:1-6

Rejection – from his own men

This has to be the bottom of the pit. This rejection, I think is the greatest wounding of all. Sure, Israel's head honcho doesn't understand him and misinterprets his motives. I think he could even take it on the chin, that the enemy doesn't trust him. But when he goes home, there is no home left because his family has been kidnapped from an act of war. The attack on their village was from enemies from yet *another* side. That is tough, but when his *own men* reject him? Those he had harboured, had taken in when they were distressed, and in debt, and discontent... when *they* turn on him, that is the hardest of all.

If we were to ask "Why?" in this moment, the whole journey would just seem kind of pointless. These men have served David for years in the wilderness, wandering around as nomadic fugitives. Finally, they get a place to call home, a place to settle, and now Ziglag is burnt and razed to the ground.

I suspect these men had also asked 'The Why' Question, and they came up with an answer. It was not an accurate answer but one that they hook onto: David is why! David is the reason they were so wounded, and they were going to stone him! That would fix everything! Obviously.

We are not told how David talked them down, but we are given an indication of the way he responded to cope with the depth of this challenge.

When I feel wounded and rejected... where do I go to find strength?

Responding to Heart Wounds

Bible Reading
1 Samuel 30:6-20

Find Strength

David's first port of call is God – finding strength in the Lord. This is a personal encounter, a personal pursuit of God's presence. He goes to God for his strength, as his refuge. He looks to God for his recovery, for his refreshment. He doesn't depend on the priest. Or the pastor. Or his men. Or his family. Or his wives. No. David takes personal responsibility for positioning himself near God's heart.

In what ways to I strengthen myself in the Lord?

Everything he has done up to this point, every time he applied this practice, that was resourcing David for what he needs now. This is perhaps the hardest challenge of all, and he goes to God. He finds strength in God's presence. There is no one else who is with him. When everything else is stripped away and there is nothing left, David seeks strength in the Lord Jehovah Elohim, the Exceeding Great and Mighty One.

I think it is noteworthy, that the darkest hour comes just before the dawn. If David had given up here, the rest would be an untold story. But he doesn't give up, even though he has no idea that the turning point is just over the rise.

What is it like to think the darkest hour comes just before the dawn?

Where have I wanted to give up... and may have also given up on the next part of the plan?

Follow God's lead

When David was strengthened, then he pauses and inquired as to what to do next. Did you notice the sequence here? David didn't dive straight into the solution, to fix the problem, as we are prone to do. He *first* seeks strength he needed to revive his spirit first, then when he was revived and stronger, then he was in a position to seek wisdom... and *then* a solution.

So, David inquires of the Lord. Abiathar the priest, was the son of Ahimelek from Nob who was martyred for helping David. He brings the ephod. The ephod was the priestly garment of worship and praise, so this suggests they have positioned and clothed themselves with a stance of praise and worship. As they cloth themselves in worship, they inquire of God for a plan. Again, there is process, a protocol; he is careful about that. No presumption.

Every other response David has engaged in prepares him for this challenge. Every song he wrote; every psalm he sang; every prayer he prayed; every lamb he protected from the lion and the bear... every challenge he rose to... from Goliath to the myriad of other battles he has fought, David knows victory is from the Lord. Without God they have no chance of winning. There is humility in this stance. There is strength and wisdom in this approach.

Do I make time to strengthen myself before I dive into solutions and fixing things?

It is in this place that the priest asks God a 'Yes-No' check. Will we? We have this idea… will we proceed? Yes or No? David hasn't come empty; now he has strength from the Lord and the Spirit of God responds, with an emphatic "*Yes!*".

Fix onto the plan

Okay! Now they have a plan. They have been excluded from the other battle with the Philistines, but now they have another battle to fight, a personal battle one that means so much more to each of these men.

They *regroup*. They *refocus* and they go after the warring tribes of the Amalekites to *retrieve* and *return* that which was taken. These men are all in: 100%. They are skilled warriors. Six hundred men in all. Two hundred of them are too exhausted to continue, and that leaves four hundred go up against a national army.

Then we notice the unusual provision of a guide – another wounded and discontent and discarded servant. Their compassion for this wounded man provides a willing defector who would take them right into the camp of the Amalekites.

They win this war. The enemy falls, except four hundred Calvary warriors on camels. That was the only remanent that got away, which was the same number of their own little army. That suggests that there was a lot of others who fell that day against David and his men. This is a victory like Gideon against the Midianites. This is another David against Goliath moment. This is another instance of God fighting battles with his people against the overwhelming to bring them through to victory.

In the end, nothing from Ziglag was lost; not one person was injured – both from of those taken from Ziglag, or in their own army. They *all* come back! That is the protection of God: when life happens. God protects! We see David rise to the full standing of an honourable commander.

The Principle of Belonging: Everyone has a place

Bible Reading
1 Samuel 30:21-31

It is significant that in a season of displacement, David advocates strongly for the principle of belonging. This is the stance, not just of an honourable commander but of an honourable king. David holds the position that he was not just taking charge of the strong and the useful, but he acknowledges that everyone has a place – even the tired and worn down. Everyone has a contribution; everyone has a way to impact and support the outcome.

How important for you is belonging as an aspect of God's kingdom?

Everyone suffers – everyone shares

This even included the distribution of the plunder of war. There is one thing to say we are in this together, but are we really? What about when it comes to the *stuff*, the plunder or war, and the rewards? Each one of those men were impacted by the raid on Ziglag. Everyone suffered; everyone did the hard yards. Even if they didn't participate on the front line, those left behind were participating by protecting the stores.

There is no record to say that the men left behind even did this, but David gave them the credit for doing so. They had a role and a place, that means they also had a share in the rewards and the spoils of war. They got an equitable share. This was unusual for this period of war and plunder: the strong prosper and the weak suffer. We see it even now... the productive are rewarded... the challenged and vulnerable are sidelined. But this is not unusual as a principle of belonging in God's Kingdom. David's heart was so aligned with God's principles, that he didn't even need to debate it. This was the right thing to do.

Have I wanted to exclude others, because their contribution doesn't seem to be part of the front-line?

So, David takes a stance that becomes a lasting ordinance, and an enduring principle for Israel as a nation. We all belong. We all get to share, and it seems that after all this, after the displacement, and wounding, and the strengthening, and the battles... that God looks down and says, "Now! *Now* you are ready. *Now* I have a King after my own heart!"

Elders acknowledged

David is a statesman. He doesn't take all the stuff for himself even though this was the plunder accumulated by the Amalekites for a whole season of many raids and battles, probably from Israel's people. David doesn't take the credit for himself even though he led the campaign. He sends all the elders of Israel, a portion of the spoils of war with a note: *"Here is a gift for you from the plunder of the LORD's enemies"*. He gives the credit to God – this was plunder from the *Lord's* enemies. Not yours; not mine. He sends the elders a portion of the spoils.

This was a lot of loot that they had acquired and rather than set up his own little kingdom... he defers to those who hold influence in Israel: the elders. David diplomatically reminds the elders that God is still fighting the battles of his people; that he is still around – a warrior, a commander, a statesman, and an anointed King... and God is still winning!

Hmm – this is an interesting point to reinforce, because while this is happening King Saul is at war fighting the Philistines... and losing! Badly losing. In fact, this battle against the Philistines, is the battle in which King Saul was killed, along with his three sons, including Jonathan.

We can now see God's hand of protection overruling in the rejection David experienced. David was not placed in a position of divided loyalties. David was not in the battle that killed his king and his best friend, Prince Jonathan. David wasn't even there. He cannot be accused of taking matters into his own hands to secure the crown. Instead, now there is a King after God's own heart... who is positioned for the next season, *without* blood on his hands.

Is there a time, where you felt things were going against you and afterwards you could see the protection of God?

Shadows of Messiah

In this story, there again are prophetic shadows of Messiah. Jesus was rejected... by his own people... the Jews. He was condemned by the enemies of Israel and occupying forces of Rome. And Jesus was rejected by his own men... not one of the twelve... who had walked and learnt from him as disciples for three years was able to stay, even to pray with him before his trial. Yet in the face of all this wounding, Jesus strengthened himself in the Lord... his prayers in Gethsemane... was the darkest hour as he sought strength to stay fixed on the goal... the biggest plan of all. The plan of Salvation... the battle to retrieve those who the enemy had stolen and taken captive.

Final Thoughts...

David was given a promise and an anointing to be King over Israel and yet for years he has been living in a wilderness. He has been rejected by his own King. Eventually he aligns himself with the neighbouring Kingdom of the Philistines, even though they are the sworn enemies of Israel. Then, when it seems like they have found a place to settle the families of his six hundred men, he is rejected again by King Achish and his army. His hometown is attacked and razed by foreign Amalekite raiders and finally his own men turn on him. Stuff happens, life happens and sometimes that stuff is not good stuff.

I remember a time when I had a miscarriage, and it was a deeply personal and sad time for me. I remember sharing that with a friend of mine. He was just starting to learn about the things of God. He asked, "Why? How can this happen when you are a healthy woman, a spiritual woman? Why would God do this to you?"
I said to him, "We live in a world broken and impacted by sin and pain. I live here and I am no more exempt from those decays in our world

than the next person. That doesn't mean God doesn't love me or that he is not with me in this."

As I looked back on that conversation, I notice God was in that response. It was something that came immediately from my gut. I didn't have to formulate a theological response. It was a reality that I knew. That situation deeply impacted me, but being aware of God's presence in that sadness helped me navigate it.

Life happens. God doesn't take control like we sometimes expect. God is not a "lawn-mower parent" who mows down everything in our path to keep things smooth. Rather he offers strength, resources, and protection in all of life situations... even the difficult and challenging times.

Unlike the rejection that occurred after protecting the sheep of Nabal, this time David goes to God for strength first. He seeks God's wisdom and guidance regarding his next move; he defers to God's timing and then he moves. Everything that was lost was restored. They found everyone had been protected and families were reunited, plus more.

This darkest hour, even though David didn't know it at the time, was the final chapter in this season of waiting in exile. In hindsight we can see these battles were right on the eve of when David's promises would be fulfilled. Now David is prepared, ready to step into being King, a King after God's heart that seeks Him first.

Prayer:

Father God, we are aware that life happens, and we understand that some of those things can be deeply troubling, and they can really wound us. But Father, we also acknowledge that you are not a lawn mower parent. Rather, you are a present parent who walks besides us, nurtures us, strengthens us, guides us, gives us wisdom, gives us courage. We ask Father that you would help us to be aware that in all life circumstances that we can go to you first, and we can strengthen ourselves in the Lord, just like David did. We ask Father God, that as we navigate life's challenges, that like David, we would give you the credit and acknowledge that the battle belongs to the Lord. Father, help us to become so practiced in these disciplines of acknowledging your presence in our lives, that when we really need it, our default will be confidence that you are with us, you love us, and our protection comes from you.

Father God, we pray for those who are navigating circumstances that are wounding them and ask that you would bind up those hurt places; that you would be their strength; you would be their comfort, that they would find rest in you. We pray for courage that once they have an understanding of a plan to move forward in your grace, that they will do so with your wisdom and strength.
In Jesus name, Amen.

7

A Worshipping Heart

Where we are...

As we continue on David's remarkable journey of being anointed as King over Israel, we have looked at some of the high-lights and low-lights as he moves towards reigning as king. This now takes us into the Second book of Samuel.

After the attack on Ziglag, David moves to Hebron. Thousands of Israelites defect from the House-of-Saul over to David. David is appointed King in Hebron. When King Saul and his sons were killed in a battle against the Philistines, King Saul's fourth son was not in that battle. His name was Ish-bosheth, and he was appointed King over Israel. So, for this time, Israel is a split Kingdom. Ish-bosheth reigns as the son of King Saul, who was the legitimate heir according to tradition. He was 40 years old, but most commentators say his name means "Son of Shame" and that he was an "*imbecile*". The commander of the army, Abner, made the decisions and Ish-bosheth operates as a puppet king. During the reign of King David in Hebron, Israel is thrown into civil war, the House of Saul against the House of David.

Eventually, with fair mix of intrigue, defection, political alliances, assignations and counter alliances, David is crowned King over all of Israel when he is thirty-seven years old. The nation is united once more. One Nation, under one king, under the one true God!

David captures Jerusalem and establishes it as the "City of David". This is a landmark conquest. Jerusalem is now the capital of Israel. David builds a palace there. Another war with the Philistines breaks out and David demonstrates that God is again fighting the battles of Israel with them.

So politically, stability is established, but David is aware that his mandate is not just a political one, it is also a spiritual one. David was not just to unite the nation together with political stability, but that, under God, they are to worship the Lord their God with all their heart, and soul, and mind. David identifies that one of the big issues is that the Ark of the Covenant is not in Jerusalem. David determines to rectify this situation.

Returning to the Presence of God

Bible Reading
2 Samuel 6:1-8

Right Purpose

We know that God has been with David, even in the wilderness. We know he is anointed with the Spirit of God. However, the understanding and revelation to this point was that God's presence presided with the Ark of the Covenant. Abinadab's household had been blessed as they were custodians of the Ark for twenty years.

David sincerely desires to bring the Ark of the Covenant back into focus, back into the centre of the culture of his people. His heart is set on the right purpose. His intent is to bring the Kingdom of Israel back into alignment. This was not just establishing the freedom and governance of the nation's people with stability, but that their spiritual health would be strengthened also. This means the presence and worship of God would be honoured and central to all matters of life. For Israel, they needed to return to their Covenant relationship with

God and that meant the expression of worship again would be centralised around the Ark of the Covenant.

Right Place

It was also right that the Ark of the Covenant be in Jerusalem. The Ark had not been at the centre of worship since the time of Eli and Samuel when the ark was captured by the Philistines. The Lord returned the ark from the temple of the Philistines however it was still not in the Tabernacle where it truly belonged. The Ark had been at the house of Abinadab, a Levite and his sons, who have caretakers of it for twenty years.

Bible Reference
1 Chronicles 13:3

The elders of Israel had not inquired of Ark at all during the reign of King Saul. The presence and wisdom of God had been left out of the governance of Israel. Now David sets about, in consultation with the elders of Israel, to bring the Ark back into the city of Jerusalem. He is bringing God back into the central place of governance of his nation.

Wrong process

In Verse 2 we are told that the Ark of Covenant, is called by *the Name, the name of the LORD Almighty*, who is enthroned between the cherubim on the ark..."

The Name of God that David uses here is Jehovah Tsaba (pronounced *Tsaw-baw*) which means *"hosts"* or *"armies"* who are organised for battle. God had given David the throne over Israel, but God was eternally enthroned, symbolically represented by his presence on the mercy seat between the cherubim of the ark of the covenant.

David has previously demonstrated a strong sense of protocol, but this time, the nature of his preparations was not attentive to what God wanted. Once David had been the commander of a Band of six hundred discontent men; now he is King with an army of over thirty thousand. The army is gathered for this momentous occasion. There were orchestras; there were choirs; there were flashing lights and smoke machines. All is going well, and then suddenly the oxen pulling the cart stumble. Abinadab's son Uzzah tries to stabilize the Ark, and he dies instantly at the hand of God

Hmm. What do you think is going on here?

We are told David becomes very angry by this! He had the right intentions; his purpose was God aligned. He had the right place: Jerusalem was the City of Peace which was now the capital of Israel. But even with all this worship and honour, and sincere effort, the ceremony is stopped mid-step.

When have I had the right idea, right motives, right place, but something hasn't gelled?

The text says that the act of Uzzah was *irreverent*: familiar and presumptuous. The Ark had been in his home for twenty years. It *also* says that after this event David developed a new depth of reverence, awe, respect and fear of God.

God is not a lucky charm; he is not an idol; he is not like the god's that the nations around them worshipped. He is The Mighty God of the "hosts-of-the-angel-armies". This ceremony is put on hold as David retreats and tries to work out what is going on. The Ark now goes into the custody of household of Obed-Edom. Obed-Edom's household is blessed – Josephus says he goes from poverty to great prosperity during the three months the Ark was in his household. Then David tries again to bring the Ark back to Jerusalem.

Bible Reading
2 Samuel 6:12-19
1 Chronicles 15:13

Directed by God

The account in Chronicles gives some indicators about what was lacking in the process that caused that ceremony to be stopped the first time. The instructions given to Moses was that the Ark was only to be transported by the hands of Levites and it was to be carried on poles.

So where did they get the idea of a cart drawn by Oxen? Perhaps it echoes back to the way that God guided the Ark back from the land of the Philistines. The Philistines had put the Ark on a new cart with unbroken oxen and God guided the oxen to the border of Israel. But this was only a retrieval plan; an oxcart was not what God had instructed – even if it was brand new and purpose built. There were to be *no* animals involved. It was *only* to be carried by Levites – people dedicated to the worship and service of God. They had deferred to a tradition and ideas that had been handed down without referring back to the word of God. In doing this, they found themselves deviating from what God had prescribed as honouring and pleasing to him.

Is it possible that some aspects of my worship is based more on tradition and not completely aligned with God's heart?

Bible Reading
1 Chronicles 15:1-4; 13-16

The Chronicles account also says that David purpose built a place for the ark of God and pitched a tent for it to house it. That also suggests to me that the first time around he hadn't really thought through where the Ark would reside. We know from 2 Chronicles 8:11 that this special tent was within the compound of the Palace. His idea was that, as soon as he could, he would build a proper temple for the Lord, one that was fitting for the worship of the Mighty God. So now David is prepared to try again. By following the directions provided by God, he again resolves to bring the Ark into Jerusalem, this time understanding more fully what is acceptable to God.

Dressed in an ephod

Bible Reference
1 Chronicles 15:27

David wears an ephod

David is dressed in a robe of fine linen as well as a linen ephod. These were the garments of praise. For this occasion – David takes off his Kingly garments – and puts on the garments of praise and worship. This was an expression of honour and worship and joy. David is not holding back. He is dancing and worshiping "with all of his might".

Worship is familiar territory for David; he regularly goes there, but this time, it is a special time of intense, focused, in-the-moment worship.

In what ways do I dress myself in a garment of praise, in order to prepare myself to enter the presence of God?

As their King, David is heading the procession; he is providing an example of what an offering of praise and worship looks like. We have witnessed how David boldly steps into battle and the people are strengthened with courage. The same principle is seen here. They witness their King who is not afraid to worship with all of his might, dancing before the Lord, without shame or hesitation.

From the top, worship will cascade down to the people. David is demonstrating what a worshiping King looks like, modelling a nation who honours God, covered with a garment of praise.

Doorway of Sacrifice

David worships and also paves the way with sacrifice. This wasn't just a sacrifice of praise and song, but he demonstrates his worshiping heart with the sacrifices of bulls and fattened calves. Instead of the bulls pulling the cart, they become *the* sacrifice. The whole trip from Odem-Edom's residence into the city of Jerusalem was about 30 km. The account says at every 6 paces, a sacrifice was made. It's not clear if that happened the whole 30 km or just for the final part of the journey as they are entering the city. Either way, this is a serious commitment of sacrifice, in money, and time, and investment. This is not half hearted. They are all in. They are paving the way with sacrifice. This means something. There is the blood of bulls and fattened calves, the best of the land.

There is the sacrifice of praise, as the music and instruments and choirs singing and playing. There is the sacrifice of worship as David danced before the Lord in the priestly robes. These are the things that provided access into the presence of God as the Ark is carried into Jerusalem.

What are the sacrifices that I make before God as I enter his presence with praise?

One thing I am learning to appreciate more and more, as I read these accounts, is that the Israelites really knew how to celebrate with style and skill before God. This attribute of excellence reflected God's heart, and this is an appropriate celebration as the Ark finally arrives in Jerusalem. It is a time of great joy, and festivity. The people are gifted with a party-pack. Yet there was one blip on the radar of this wonderful time of celebration.

I remember participating in a group and one of the people in the group was having a difficult time. It was agreed that we were going to pray for her. I thought, "Oh, good! This is my zone," and I internally prepared. We stood in a circle; we held hands; there was a pause... and then immediately, everyone in unison recited the Lord's Prayer.
"Oh no!" I thought, "This is not right! We can do better than this." Then I had a check: this was the way they were lifting this person up in prayer. Just because the words were not injected with 'Halleluiahs' and

'Amens', that my Pentecostal culture preferred, it doesn't prevent God from meeting this person's need in the way that was best.

Then, I had another check. I remembered sitting with a member of our church as he was telling me his story. He spoke about how he had a medical emergency and could feel himself dying. The only way he knew how to reach out to God in that moment was to prayer the Lord's Prayer. So, in the fading weakness of that deathly moment he prayed, "Our Father, who art in Heaven..." God met him in that moment: saved his life, healed him, and drew him into our church family.

As that prayer circle drew to a close, I had to apologize to God for judging other people's form of worship.

Bible Reading
2 Samuel 6:16, 20-23

Blessing to berated

David establishes the role of all the priests; the Levites are in place to direct the worship of God appropriately and then David returns to his own household to bless them. He steps back into the role of husband and father. He goes there to impart a blessing but instead he is hit with a barrage of scorn.

His wife, Michal, spits out an onslaught of contempt, judgement, and disdain over David. After a highpoint, a victory, a spiritual highlight of worshipping God, comes an assault that drives in hard to cut and wound.

Have I ever caught myself despising someone else's style of worship or the nature of their ministry expression?

What Michal says goes to the core of David's identity. It is a dark contrast to his heart of worship that she presents. There are a few things I note about Michal's verbal vomit:

It was not factual:

David wasn't dancing around naked as she accuses him of doing. Even though this has become the perception of this parade into Jerusalem. David was dressed in the same uniform as the Levites with the addition of the ephod. What he had done, was to take *off* the robes of his office – his Kingly garments and he replaced them with garments of praise. What she said was based on Michal's opinion of acceptable appearances.

She is using an old template:

Michal had grown up as a princess in the palace of her father King Saul. She had a particular understanding of what a King looked like, how a King carried himself. That perception was based on Saul's template. But David is rewriting the template of Israel's kings; he is doing it differently; he is doing it in a Godly way. He is doing it from a heart that follows after God.

She curses and berates her husband.

Michal declares that all David had achieved was public humiliation and disrespect as a common, uncouth man, (even a despised shepherd?).

She is challenging God's appointment.
She is challenging his style of governance.
She is challenging his relationship with God.
She is also challenging his place in her household. *"I'm a princess; You are a common shepherd. This is a disgrace and its humiliating. You need to lift your game!"* Notice how back-to-front that is.

Bold Focus

David does not hesitate. He does not submit to her scorn or her berating. He does not allow her to steal away this wonderful milestone in their nation with her judgement and attitude.

He holds on to what he knows.
He knows there is no shame in worshiping God.
He knows that God has appointed him.
He knows that God is his judge, not Michal, nor the media, or social websites.
He knows that there is even a level of discernment in the populace that is missing from Michal's lens, and he makes some very bold *"I will* statements..."

"*I will*" statements

"I will" statements are a great way to embed our intention through declaration... to hone our focus. We often end a small group discussion, with a round-table of "I will's..."

> *What am I taking away from this exchange?*
> *What is my intention to move or shift or reaffirm?*
> *What do I intend to do with this?*

Here David makes quite a line-up of "*I will* statements":

> *I will* celebrate before the LORD!
> *I will* become even more undignified than this!
> *I will* be humiliated in my own eyes!

I will be held in honour!

David knows he is on track, and he is not going to be detoured, or derailed by her judgement.

What bold "I will" statements can I make today?

Barrenness

There is no mention of repentance or shame that Michal experienced from her arrogant outburst. Rather, there is a very sobering note regarding the consequences of Michal's bitter exchange. There is a hardness in her heart that continues to despise – not only David, but the things of God.

What is observed is that there was a barrenness that pervaded Michal's life. In this era, that meant not having children. I am not making the inference that infertility is a reproach from God. There are many reasons why this sadness visits some families. Although there is nothing that explicitly says this, I suspect that David excluded Michal from his bedroom from this point forward.

There are many commentaries that draw the link in this story between, Michal's insolent judgement, her despising heart, and the lack of fruitfulness that she experienced in her life. Judging and despising another, whether it be their life and standing before God, whether it be their call, or their ministry, or their worship-style as inadequate or inferior or misdirected, that becomes very dodgy ground.

Insolence, and despising others, does not reflect the nature and honour of God. A consequence of that hardness in our heart, may be unfruitfulness and barrenness in our lives. The God who blesses, who is gracious, shows loving kindness, will forgive our wrong-doing if we have a heart that repents and aligns with him, when we desire to worship God and reverence him. But God cannot work with a heart that despises, when there is a hardness there. That hardness will not bear fruit.

Bible Reading
2 Samuel 7:18-24

David's Prayer:

This is a beautiful prayer which David offered, as God makes a covenant with David as King over Israel. There is no arrogance, or disdain in these words. His heart is soft with worship as David sits before the presence of the Lord in the Place of Meeting. There is an acknowledgement of that all that had been achieved was through the grace and favour of God.

Nathan the prophet tells David that although his desire to build a temple for the Lord is an honourable one, it would not be for him to do this. God had appointed his successor this role, but God shows David that he is not missing out. His influence is enduring... flowing down through the generations.

What has God appointed me to accomplish, and what has he appointed to someone else to do?

David prophetically declares that God's promise to establish Israel as God's own people is becoming a reality, not just in his lifetime but this would continue down through the generations from his line.

We know that Jesus was ultimately the highest fulfilment of God's promise to David. Jesus came as the last and final king from the house of David. No longer would people need to offer a sacrifice every six steps, to enter into the presence of God. Jesus was the sacrifice that became the doorway into the joyful presence of God. The Lord was true to his word, true to his covenant to David and true to his desire to redeem all people to himself and we see that promise as we look into the face of Jesus.

Final Thoughts...

It has been fifteen long years from when David was anointed by Samuel as a fifteen-year-old, to when he takes the throne in Hebron. Seven years later David has been crowned King over all Israel. Now he is in a position to bring the Ark of the Covenant – the Ark that carried the presence of God... into Jerusalem. He does this, demonstrating by example, what the worshiping heart of a King looks like. As he does, there is one person who stands apart and distains his worship. All she sees is David's lack of dignity.

I remember having a couple conversations around a situation that occurred in a small country evangelical church. The pastor was praying one day for a lady, and she went down in the spirit.
I was aware that God had been moving in that church in Spirit-filled ways during that season. I spoke to the pastor afterwards and he said he was surprised, even shocked, by what had happened. God's Holy Spirit had not moved like that when he had prayed for someone before. It was new and uncomfortable for him.

Not long after that, I was speaking with someone else who had been there and he brought up this incident. He used phrases like "grandstanding"; "prideful"; "putting it on"; "intentionally trying to impress people". While he was talking, I remembered this story of David and Michal. I knew that from the pastor's perspective that was not at all what was in his heart.

I have had another conversation; this one was from the other side of the coin. A lady had married into a very strong Pentecostal family, but she said she felt judged and berated by her family as a second-rate, second-class Christian, because her expression of worship and prayer were not like her husband's or her in-laws, since she had not received the gift of tongues.

We need to be careful with our heart, so we don't become arrogant, or hardened, or critical, just because something is uncomfortable for us. Perhaps that discomfort is related to how it is different to what we understand of the work of God. If something is uncomfortable for us, then before God, we need to work through that. It maybe that we are discerning something that is skewed and unbalanced, or it may be that God is doing something different and extraordinary. When we harden our heart with criticism, that will lead to a barrenness in our lives that will not bear fruit.

God loves us all. He is an inclusive, gracious, patient, loving God who embraces all sorts of faith-expressions. Our responsibility is to check our heart, so it stays in a place of worship before him. To worship God with all of our strength. To love God with all of our heart. To sacrifice generously as we love other people and to allow others the freedom to do the same. This is part of what made David a King whose heart worshiped The Mighty God of the Hosts of the Angel Armies.

Prayer:

Father God, it is such a privilege to know that Jesus has paved the way through sacrifice for us to be able to enter your presence. We are so grateful that we don't have enter into your presence, every six steps, by sacrificing a bull and a calf. We are also aware Father God that you are the great and mighty God of the hosts of the angel armies. We know that you are above all, and in all, and it is our desire to worship you in spirit and in truth, with all of our heart, and all of our mind, and all of our being. But sometimes Father God we fall so short of that. Help us to be mindful, not to stand in an arrogant place, as other people are walking their own journey with you. Help us to be people who will lift them up and encourage them, support them to step into a greater awareness of who you are and what you have available for them. Father, help us not to be people who stare from the window and distain what is happening. May we be people who are able to enter in, and sing, and celebrate, for the good things you that are doing! You are the God who dwells with your people, and we are so grateful that you are present with us. Father God, we want to be a people who includes you in the centre of everything: that same idea that David wanted to represent by bringing the Ark into Jerusalem. Father God, may we be so mindful of your presence with us as we walk into this week.
In Jesus name, Amen.

8

A Forgiving Heart

Where we are...

In 2 Samuel 8:15 we have a very succinct summary of David's impact as King: *"David reigned over all Israel; and David executed judgment and justice unto all his people..."*

King David has established a united Israel. One Nation, under one king... under the one true God! He reigns justly. He rules rightly. Everyone, all his people experienced this justice.

He unites the nation together with political stability under God; they worship the Lord their God with all their heart and soul and mind. But there is another side to David's reign... it was not just a rule of justice and rightness... but he also governed with mercy and forgiveness, and that is what we are going to consider today.

I remember a public situation, when a pastor appreciated something, I had done. Having my contribution acknowledged was nice, but he went further. He told everyone he was going to buy me a box of chocolates as a gesture of his gratitude.
My daughter was not very old, and she became excited. I cautioned her gently. "Just be aware Sweetheart, that this might not happen..."
"But he said..." she defended.
"Yes, I know Honey... but let's just wait and see..."
Perhaps it was the fact that now my daughter was watching that this became a 'thing' for me. I really wanted this person to follow through on what he had said. It was not actually about the chocolates, but a

pattern I noticed emerging. I could go and buy chocolates any time. I even made a resolution that if I did ever receive these chocolates, I would pass them on to the other people who were helping me at the time. But I was interested in the follow-through. Would that happen? I didn't really expect that it would. Yet when it didn't, I was disappointed but not surprised. Still, I thought it might be appropriate to give this person the benefit of the doubt. So, I spoke to him about his promise and his response was: "You should have reminded me!"
I watched as he wrote a note in his dairy.
I still haven't seen those Thankyou-Chocolates.
This passing incident challenged me on my own capacity to follow through.

David was a man with follow-through. Today's account is a wonderful heart-felt story of follow-through... and it also one of generous forgiveness and grace. It is certainly something for us to aspire to.

As matters of State stabilize, David identifies that there was a matter that he not addressed fully and this related to the covenant of friendship that he had made with Jonathan.

Bible Reading
1 Samuel 20:14-15

David had vowed faithfulness to Jonathan, and he now has a conviction that he had not been actively engaging in this commitment. It was passive and left to circumstances. David determines to rectify this situation and to fulfil his vow to Jonathan.

Bible Reading
2 Samuel 4:4
2 Samuel 9:1-13

Mephibosheth – the Unseen son

Mephibosheth was the grandson of a king and the son of a prince. But now that King Saul is dead and his throne is overturned, his linage is a shameful connection. More than that, it is a dangerous acknowledgement. Mephibosheth has grown up in hiding.

The traditions of succession in ancient kingdoms were to eradicate the opposition and rivals to the throne to secure one's reign. Jonathan knew this. This was Saul's driving motivation for most of his rule. Yet Jonathan also believed God's word and destiny over David's life. He knew that enmity between them would be politically inevitable. This was not just perpetuating Saul's plot against David, but when David rose to be King, then David would need to politically guard his own throne. Often that meant innocent assignations. Jonathan's vow and covenant with David was to pre-empt and forestall that normal chain of events.

Mephibosheth was a five-year-old child when news of his father's death in battle against the Philistines came to the palace. This was a sweeping defeat, not just the King, but three of the direct heirs in line to the throne also died that day. This defeat was not just on the battlefield. It extends to the reigning establishment and throughout the whole kingdom. Panic breaks out. Everyone in the palace feared for their lives. They are literally running for their lives. Everything changes. Instability. Alarm. Uncertainty. Fear. They flee and Mephibosheth goes from living in privilege in the palace, to living in hiding.

Unfit for public life

The nurse who was designated to look after Jonathan's son, hears the news of the battle, grabs Mephibosheth, and flees. In the panic, she stumbles. Accounts outside the bible says[v] the child was dropped from the nurse's shoulders. That is a long drop. He acquired terrible injuries to both feet. There is no provision for surgery, no physiotherapy. He cannot even rest. They are fugitives. Nerve damage, mal-alignment and deformity become Mephibosheth's reality. He grows up to live life as a cripple... lame in both feet. He is dependant; he is immobile. Mephibosheth is a pathetic tribute to what is left of the royal house of Saul. His Uncle, Ish-bosheth, was known as the 'Imbecile King'. He reigned for a few years, before he was assassinated in his bed. That was a matter that David was furious about; but it happened. Mephibosheth's mentally capacity was fine, however his life has been hidden in shame, not just because of his heritage but because of his physical deformity and disability. He was unfit to participate in normal life, much less a life of royalty.

Undeserved restoration

David however has not forgotten his word to Jonathan. He had the integrity to follow-through on his word. Even when, there was no one to hold him to account. Even when, there was no social expectation for him to do anything different to what he had already been doing.

Do I keep my word, regardless of whether other people remember it or not?

He faithfully keeps his word to his friend Jonathan. David has no idea if the assignation of Ish-bosheth ended the line of Saul completely. So, he sets out to investigate the matter more thoroughly. He summons Ziba – one of Saul's stewards, who discloses there was one remaining son of Jonathan, Mephibosheth – now a young man. Mephibosheth is 25 years younger than David.

Suddenly, this life of shame has been turned around. He is given a second chance. David restores to Mephibosheth, all the lands of his father's inheritance that were part of the tribe of Benjamin.

Is there some grace act that I need to follow-up and address?

As a cripple Mephibosheth has no income or capacity for income. Now he has land and the resources of his grandfather's steward to provide for him. Not only that, David also reassures him that his life is not in danger, rather he is going to be respected with favour. He is given a designation of honour: eating at the King's table. This is generous, lavish, extravagant gesture! As a young man, he is treated as a son of David's House.

This is Jubilee. Jubilee is the grace provision in the law of Moses that every fifty years; after seven cycles of seven years, freedom, land and inheritances are to be restored to those who have had it taken away. Slaves and prisoners would be freed; debts would be forgiven, and the mercies and kindness of God would be demonstrated.

Mephibosheth is experiencing Jubilee grace, whether or not it was marked in the timestamp of the Jubilee decree. This was his experience! He *was* marked with shame... yet his humble position was raised to royalty. He *was* disinherited... but his family's property was generously returned. He *was* living in hiding... but he was adopted into the household of David as if he was a son. What a beautiful picture of God's forgiveness and grace in practice. Nothing was earned. Nothing was expected. Nothing was merited. Yet David lavishly extends the boarders of his household to include Mephibosheth, and we see that

Mephibosheth stays in Jerusalem and becomes part of the House of David.

What is it like to remind myself that I have received generous mercy like Mephibosheth?

But this is not the last that we hear of Mephibosheth. If we fast-forward many years to when David is 60 years old, we see that things have gone badly in the Kingdom.

David's third son, Absalom, is 30 years old: he is handsome and bold, and very vain. He obsessively loves his hair... and he obsessively loves everyone noticing it. Absalom was born to one of David's wives, who was a princess of the King of Geshur, which is the area of modern-day Golan Heights.

Absalom makes a bid for the crown, against his father. Absalom leads an insurrection against David... and crowns himself king. Many Israelites' defect to Absalom and David is forced to evacuate Jerusalem to save the lives of his faithful subjects. David leaves Jerusalem by one gate, while Absalom and his troops are coming in another, to take over the palace.

Bible Reading
2 Samuel 16:1-4

Absalom's Betrayal & Slander

The context of this encounter is massive betrayal. David was Absalom's father, but Absalom was only loyal to his own promotion. Absalom was devious and manipulative and he doesn't play fair. He progressively slandered his father over the years, positioning himself for the throne. He suggested and whispered: "David is too busy... David doesn't care... But I do..." The kingdom was rife with subterfuge and intrigue. It must have been difficult to discern who was honest, who was sincere, who was faithful... and who was not.

What has been my response when I experienced betrayal and slander?

Even as David is retreating from the city – there is a Benjaminite (the same tribe as King Saul) named Shimei who follows along the ridge beside the road as the line of their company is leaving. Shimei is yelling curses, and slander, pelting rocks at David and his group from the ridge.

Mephibosheth betrays

As David is leaving Jerusalem, he meets Ziba, the steward from the House of Saul who had been put in charge of Mephibosheth's affairs. We know Ziba was also a Benjaminite – also from the Tribe of Saul. Mephibosheth is not with him. Ziba is going the wrong way, he is going back to Jerusalem.

David asks a few pertinent questions and Ziba tells him that Mephibosheth has betrayed David. After all the grace that was shown to him! Mephibosheth, Ziba says, was hopeful of re-establishing King Saul's throne! Ziba sums it up: "Mephibosheth is staying in Jerusalem, because he thinks, 'Today the Israelites will restore to me my grandfather's kingdom.'" The gifts that Ziba brings David, including the donkeys to ride on, must have been a relief. Someone is still faithful, thinking of him, has his back. Ziba was given authority by David, to take Saul's lands for himself and his own family, instead of caretaking for a lame turncoat.

Forgiveness is hard

This is a moment of great shame and humiliation. The climate is betrayal. A whole nation is turning. In this moment – victories don't matter. In this moment – Goliaths don't matter. In this moment – past matters governed with justice and fairness don't matter. In this moment, acts of grace and forgiveness don't matter either. Our past cannot be used like a trophy cabinet displaying victories to get us through the challenges of now.

Bible Reference
2 Samuel 16:12

How does David respond?

Forgiveness is hard. We have to walk it out in the present and the choice to walk in grace is not an easy one. It is harder when we are living in the consequences of these betrayals.

Bible Reading
2 Samuel 15: 23-30

This event has been described by R. T. Kendall[vi] as David's "finest hour". Not his grandest, not his most famous... but the place that profoundly defines a man. When there is nothing left, how do we respond? David tells Zadok the priest to return the Ark of the Covenant to Jerusalem where it belongs. He throws himself on the mercy, loving kindness and grace of God. It is up to God now. What happens, will be and can *only* be from the hand of God. And David humbly yields to the wisdom, grace and mercy of God.

So, David leaves Jerusalem in mourning. He is reliant on the forgiveness, and faithfulness of God. If restoration happens, first and foremost it is God who will restore David to his covenant blessing.

Actually, it *was* not long before the throne was restored to David. Ironically it is Absalom's vain attachment to his hair, that became his undoing. His big hair gets tangled in a tree, his horse just kept going, and he was left dangling there captured. Absalom is killed and David returns to Jerusalem to pull this divided Kingdom back together. Let's look at what happens as David is met by the people of Jerusalem as he returns as King.

Leniency

Bible Reading
2 Samuel 19:21-30

How does David respond?

Just prior to this passage, one of the faithful followers of David wanted to gift Shimei with a sword and cut off his head to silence his profanities. His desire to execute was to faithfully avenge David's honour, for the shame and slander he inflicted on David as they were leaving Jerusalem. This is the nature of light versus dark; grace versus condemnation. David's capacity for forgiveness and restoration is being revealed. This mercy was not earned. Not expected. Not merited. Shimei is not executed. He is given leniency.

Listening

Mephibosheth is also given a hearing as to why he didn't faithfully follow David as he evacuated Jerusalem. David listens. He hears Mephibosheth's account and something is revealed. Mephibosheth is not the traitor, but Ziba was taking advantage of the political situation to secure his own family's position. King David has already turned Mephibosheth's property over to Ziba. The reversal of this bequest is not completely made, but there is another edict. Now they would share the land of Saul's house between them. A 50-50 split.

Commentaries suggest that David is probably not sure of the true story or that he is hedging his bets when every alliance is needed to re-establish his throne. This seems like an unsatisfactory resolution for me: Ziba the steward walks away with half a king's estate by manipulation, corruption, and betrayal. Mephibosheth loved David well and this seems pretty unfair to me.

Then something occurred to me... isn't this the nature of grace and forgiveness? It can seem unfair. Nothing was earned. Nothing was expected. Nothing was merited and yet David lavishly extends the mercy of his judgement to include Ziba... even when Ziba was lining his own pockets and doesn't deserve it. David doesn't exclude Ziba out of mercy and forgiveness.

CS Lewis said this...
*"Everyone says forgiveness is a lovely idea,
Until he has something to forgive..."* [vii]

I think what makes this story exceptional... is the wonderful response of Mephibosheth.

Loving

Mephibosheth's response to the tragedy in David's family, torn apart by political conspiracy... is love. Mephibosheth has been in mourning since the day David left the palace. This was extended period of personal neglect... to demonstrate his distress. He was scruffy and unkept. It is evident that Mephibosheth had not at all disregarded the mercy and love bestowed on him as a son adopted into his household. There were no displaced ambitions to be raised to the throne. Mephibosheth has been faithful in his love and regard for David.

The 'stuff' Mephibosheth had been given, meant nothing to him, while David was deposed by his rebellious son. It meant even less now that David was restored as King, safe, back in Jerusalem. Mephibosheth would rather know that David was home, safe, and appointed in his rightful place. He would rather have nothing to call his own, as long as David was safe. That was far better, than quibbling over his inheritance, even for the things that Ziba had deceitfully acquired.

This is the heart of love and forgiveness. This is seeing with a heart of faithfulness. That was the heart of Mephibosheth's father, Jonathan. This is his heart of love towards David, who had adopted him as his son. In this moment we can see Mephibosheth had acquired so much more than the estates of his grandfather! I think another expression of grace in the story of Mephibosheth is that we are told Mephibosheth does have a son of his own. So, Jonathan's line continues and does not end on the battlefield. Grace restores and forgives and extends mercy. There is a prayer of forgiveness that David has written as a Maskil, a psalm:

Bible Reading
Psalm 32

David understands the blessing of forgiveness.

Final Thoughts...

David demonstrates by example... what the forgiving heart of a King looks like and there was one person who David lavishly extends the boarders of his household to include. Even though nothing was earned. Nothing was expected. Nothing was merited.

When we were planning for our overseas holiday, we chose to go to Spain. A lot of people said to me before we left... "Why Spain... like... that's an odd choice."
And I would shrug... and say... "Oh... I don't know. It is a country with a rich Christian heritage... lots of history and it's kind of different. It just appeals."
While we were in Barcelona, we went through the Citadel of the Sacred Family – Basílica de la Sagrada Família. The amazing architecture and artistic expression of the Gospel story blew me away! It was every bit incredible as we were led to believe. As we leaving the tour and walking down the sweeping steps outside, I had a profound moment with God. His Holy Spirit washed over me, and he spoke to me and said, "This is why you came to Spain. Remember how you asked me to see this in person... well, this is my gift to you."

And then in a flash I saw myself sitting in a dentist waiting room reading a National Geographic magazine... mesmerised by the Basílica de la Sagrada Família... turning the pages, immersed in its artistic architecture and its incredible spiritual symbolism. And I saw myself talking to God... "Father, there is not much on the globe that I think that I would really like to go and see in person... but this... this... I would really like to see this myself one day. In person. That would be amazing."

Oh. Wow!

I had forgotten I had even had that conversation... but God did not. God is a God who follows through. He extravagantly lavishes grace on his people – not earned, not expected, not merited.

Perhaps this is another aspect that made David... a man after God's own heart. He followed-through... even when no one was holding him to account, and he did it lavishly... extravagantly! He did the same when extending forgiveness. He didn't hold himself to the political standard, or the military standard, or the social-media standard. He held himself to the standard expressed and demonstrated by God. "Blessed is the one who is forgiven."

This has echoes of Jesus the Messiah from the linage of David. He restores and lavishes grace on us even when we don't deserve it. This is part of what made David a King whose heart was aligned with God, he was able to forgive and extend mercy.

Prayer:

Father God, I thank that you are a faithful, generous forgiving God. That you don't hold us to what we deserve or what the social standard might be. But that you give us your grace with such generous, generous

forgiveness. We thank you that you have called us in to be part of your household, you haven't left us hiding in the byways but that you have brought us in, to feast at your table. We ask Father God, that we would be people who can step into that same like-mindedness of your Spirit, that we would be generous people of follow through, generous people of forgiveness, generous people of lavish generosity and grace. Father that wherever you have positioned us that we would be people who would regard our relationships with the mindset of your Son and that we would be people after your own heart in these matters.
In Jesus name Amen.

9

A Repentant Heart

Where we are...

Last week we found a summary of King David's reign over Israel: a king who reigned with justice and who did right for all his people. (2 Samuel 8:15). As matters of state stabilize there is a certain rhythm that develops in the life of the Israelites. With all of David's battles and victories, peace is not yet achieved. David is a man of war. He still has to fight for peace, to maintain peace. He is working towards peace, but it isn't happening yet.

There was one particular place where we lived, we were caretaking a church property and we had access to some communal spaces. I there one evening after I had finished my shower, I put my toiletry bag on the table. I felt God say, "Put away your toiletry bag".
I stood there and argued with him. I didn't want to. I wanted to claim my right to use this space the way I wanted to use it. I was tired and I didn't want to be bothered. But, in the morning, when I went to have a shower... my toiletry bag was gone, and I knew exactly where I had left it!
I understood then that the things God asks of us... is for my good... not just to test me or irritate me. The same is for other boundaries God puts in place, they exist for my protection... not just to exert control over me, or to keep me supressed, or to deprive me of my freedom.
God loves us and has given us Christian moral principles to protect us and to lead us to our best lives. In today's story we see David cross some significant moral boundaries, and the consequences of those choices had lasting impacts.

Bible Reading
2 Samuel 11:1

There is an annual cycle of raiders coming in against Israel, we've met those before as well. That cycle doesn't abate. It seems this is the way that the tribal people of the Ammonites and Amalekites survive. They raid other people's work and resources. It is an annual event, predictable as the seasons.

Chapter 10 gives detail of an escalated heated feud between Israel and the Ammonites. As the Ammonite prince is crowned king when his father died, David reaches out to him in diplomacy, but they capture the delegation that David sends, humiliates them by shaving off half their beards, and cut up their robes so their buttocks were exposed. Sounds like a schoolies' prank, but this was humiliating and shameful treatment. It was definitively throwing down the gauntlet in an act of defiance, declaring war. That's what happens: war was declared; the battle was huge. The victory was great.

This time, the war was meant to be the last action needed to clean up this mess. This time, the forces of Ammon were going to be eliminated. The idea was to go out "in full force" to destroy the Ammonites for good. Their strategy involves a siege, which can go on for a long time. Some ancient sieges recorded in scripture go on for years... not just a season of months. Perhaps this strategy of a siege is why David is not on the front line this time. He's been out on the battlefield for an extended period of time. This time, he stays home.

Most commentaries suggest David was shirking his responsibility by staying in Jerusalem. Getting soft, taking it easy... an act of self-indulgence, dulling the edge of his commitment to duty, getting complacent.

Hmm, perhaps.

We know that later-on down the track, after David was nearly killed in battle, the elders refuse to allow David to go into active war again, "so the lamp of Israel will not be extinguished" (2 Samuel 21:17). But this is not the case here.

Perhaps there are matters of state that needed attention, and David didn't feel another extended period of absence, that a siege might incur, could be justified. Perhaps David has built so much confidence in his troupes that this kind of delegation is legitimately reasonable now. He has a list of Mighty Men – men of outstanding military capacity that are recognised and honoured for their acts of valour, and significant contributions to battles and victories. Whatever the rationale, he stays behind. I don't think the "why" he stayed behind in Jerusalem is as important, as to "how" he manages that time. *That* is definitely an issue.

We know David is a warrior at heart and while the army is away, he gets restless and his inability, (or unwillingness), to manage his behaviour well, causes a whole lot of problems...

Bible Reading
2 Samuel 11:2-5

The story of Bathsheba – Starts with Mighty Men

Bathsheba lives in the proximity of the palace precinct; her home is close by. She is identified very specifically as the daughter of Eliam and the wife of Uriah. These were people whom David knew. He knew them well. Both of these names are listed in that honours roll of Mighty Men – warriors of outstanding valour and victories.

Bible Reference
2 Samuel 23:8-39

This is a list of David's 37 valiant Mighty Men. Verse 34 names Eliam, son of Ahithophel the Gilonite. Verse 39 names Uriah. This means, both Bathsheba's father and husband are off fighting in this war.

More than adultery

Eliam – Bathsheba's father was the son of Ahithophel the Gilonite. Apart from the Jewish tendency to be very particular about linage, why is this information important? It is significant because Ahithophel – Bathsheba's grandfather, was one of David's close advisors. Later, when Absalom turns against his father and tries to take the throne, it is Ahithophel who becomes one of the main consultants who moves to betray David and promotes Absalom's bid for the throne. Ahithophel is known as the betrayer of David, a type of Judas. In Psalm 41:9 David writes a prayer disclosing that one of his very close and trusted friends has turned against him. It is quite accepted that David is referring to Ahithophel. Perhaps the seeds of Ahithophel's betrayal that occurred during Absalom's take-over, were planted right here. Actions have consequences. The first betrayal occurred at the hand of David: he slept with his granddaughter! And... he did that while the rest of the nation was at war!

Have I ever let the betrayal of those who have acted against my family grow into a harvest of betrayal of my own?

This was an act of great presumption. The sin of David was not just adultery, but the *sin of presumption*. Adultery is an act of the flesh. *Presumption* is a condition of the heart and that goes much deeper than having a lustful affair. David presumed he could meet his needs in a way that was outside God's guidelines. David has a lot of wives. We aren't given a specific number, although eight are named in scripture. It is assumed that he married others, but exact number is unknown[viii]. Regardless, that is still a lot of beautiful women who loved him. He could have found a willing participant to deal with his sleeplessness, or boredom, or anxiety, or whatever was going on. Yet he *presumed* he could get away with this and no one would know. He *presumed* that no one else would be impacted. He *presumed* that this would not come back and bite him. But we know that it all starts to unravel.

Monthly purification

The first clue comes as we are told that Bathsheba was attending to her monthly purification rituals.

Bible Reference
Leviticus 15: 19-29

In Leviticus, there are instructions about counting off a specific amount of time after a period, washing clothes, bathing all over and abstinence. This is what Bathsheba was doing when David saw her. I'm not going to get into why she was on her rooftop doing this. As far as she knows,.. all the men are at war. She is alone; it is at night; they don't have indoor plumbing. To me it doesn't seem terribly inappropriate. I don't buy into the idea that she was intentionally being promiscuous and offering an advertisement. But what is *not* okay is that she said "yes", when David summoned her. She didn't stand up like Abigail and pull David back to what was the better choice. This was her sin of presumption as well. If we know anything about female biology: the timing of the

Jewish women's exclusion for their monthly period, and then after their purification obligations meant that they were right at the peak of their ovulating cycle when they finished these rites. Of course she was going to get pregnant. And that is what happens. So how does David respond to this news?

Bible Reading
2 Samuel 11:6-15

Uriah's Honour Stands – David compromises

I notice how Uriah does not loosen his hold on what he understands is honourable. Bathsheba's integrity was compromised while her husband's stays true and I wonder why this isn't a caution for David, who, to this point has demonstrated an impeccable sense of honour. If David does get an internal check, he ignores it, and now he channels all of his creative energy into getting Uriah to go home and have sex with his wife. That would solve everything: the baby will be presumed to be Uriah's, and David will not be found out. The lie here is that 'what I do is just about me and the other person'. That is never the case. There are always ripples that impact people that are around us, that we cannot even imagine.

Cover up

What has happened to the matters of the kingdom that needed his attention? What about his work, his responsibilities, the war? Right now, all that is completely off David's radar. Now his focus is consumed about being in the clear. The process of cover-up, spirals and gets more complicated, and he goes deeper and deeper. David crosses the line again and again and it seems that there are no more flags or checks in his spirit. Those closest to him become complicit in this mess. Right from the first messenger who went to Bathsheba's house, they don't question him, or check-in with him. Even Joab, his commander, who is quite open and straight with David at other times, lets it go or if they did say anything, David is deaf to their advice.

Corruption sets in

It is true that David holds a role of authority, but he is not above the laws of God, and he *is* going down a very dark path. This is a very sober reminder that it doesn't matter who we are, at any time we can open the door on something that spoils and corrupts the good things in our lives. This was not just about the adultery, but it was the process of a spiralling corruption that led directly to the murder of one of his most trusted and honourable commanders.

As we read through this account, by all appearances Uriah died in active duty in the course of his military responsibilities. But God is not fooled; He calls it for what it is. Uriah was *murdered*. David accomplished what Saul tried to do to him, over and over again. Death by the enemies' sword.

I notice that Bathsheba, even though she appropriately mourns her husband, and marries David after that is completed, yet throughout scripture she continues to be referred to as Uriah's wife. Not David's.

Bible Reference
Matthew 1:6

In the gospel of Matthew, in the linage of Messiah, Bathsheba is listed, not by name, but by her marriage to Uriah. She is remembered as Uriah's wife, first and foremost. Yet rather than this whole thing going underground, God sends the prophet Nathan, to David.

Bible Reading
2 Samuel 12:1-14

Nathan's visit: A parable of injustice

It appears that Nathan is relating the account of a situation that is quite unjust. David interprets this as a real live circumstance that Nathan has come to present. Actually, Nathan is offering a relatable parable, a representation of what has happened, in a way that will allow David to hear.

Jesus did the same thing: he often told a story to communicate truth. David's defensiveness is not activated. He listens with the objectivity of a man who is expected to make a ruling over this case.

Who are the trusted Nathans in my life?

Incensed

Without hesitation or deliberation, David is incensed at the injustice of what happened to the man with the one little ewe-lamb. He activates a judgement – this is wrong! He clearly identifies the problem: Hard, callous, no pity. He delivers a sentence: the man must die! He demands restitution: he must repay four times over! Then, in those famous words, Nathan delivers the punch line to the parable: *"You are that man!"*.

Suddenly David is confronted with his sin, his hardness, his callousness, his lack of pity and the very words of his own judgement are now spoken out against himself. David stands before the prophet Nathan and God, as a man openly found guilty, charged and condemned from his own mouth. God did not have to bang the gavel, because David has already identified his guilt, and he has already identified the appropriate way to administer justice in this case.

Impacts

Everything Nathan relayed to David is true. God had been generous abundantly so. God had protected him and delivered him over and over again. Yet Nathan describes David's sin – not as sex, not as an affair, but as *despising the word of the Lord*. It was presumption to think that God would not mind; that David would not be found out, that David could despise God's nature, and it would not matter.

God is a God of justice, of what is right, of what is good... and what David did was not just, was not right and not good. God is holy, righteous, honourable and we see how, even in the face of all this, God extends mercy.

The sentence David spoke over himself is taken away. Nathan says quite clearly God will not execute the sentence that he had spoken out. David is granted mercy. He is forgiven. He would not die but that does not mean there are no impacts for the choices that he makes:

Here are a few of the consequences that Nathan identified would become part of David's heartache:

'The baby would die': I don't believe the baby is paying David's sin-price. I don't believe an innocent baby is retribution for David's bad behaviour. I don't use that lens, rather, the painful impact of this brokenness would start being experienced straight away.

'A sword would not depart from his house': We've already spoken about the uprising of his son Absalom to pursue this throne, and the civil war that he led against David. At least three of David's sons died prematurely in gory circumstances.

'What was done in secret would be made public': Absalom literally slept with his father's wives in public – on the roof of the palace – the very place where David walked when he saw Bathsheba and sent for her to share his bed. It is not all that surprising that it was Ahithophel Bathsheba's grandfather, who advised Absalom to do this act of defiance to establish his throne as king.

Bible Reading
2 Samuel 16:21-22

What I notice is that David doesn't kill Nathan for this message of grief and accountability. That was something King Saul was inclined to do. David recognises the truth in Nathan's words as a message from God. He acknowledges his bloodguilt, he confesses his sin, and asks for God's forgiveness and mercy, and he doesn't minimise the weight of the grace that has been given to him.

Here is a prayer of confession that David has written as a psalm:

Bible Reading
Psalm 51

David is fully dependent on God, *"Grant me a willing spirit,"* he cries. "God, without you I can't do this! God, without your great compassion, restoration, the cleansing I need in my life is not possible!" There is no hint of presumption in this prayer. David is taking nothing for granted. Not anymore.

Yes – he got off course, yet God in his grace, steers him back to true north and that is the beauty and mercy of this story.

Where do I need grace to cover past failures that haunt me?

Where do I need grace to restore present failures that can corrode me?

Where do I need grace to be free from the fear of future failure that can immobilize me?

Final Thoughts...

David gets off track. Really off track. Yet the story of David and Bathsheba is a profound narrative of grace. Despite the pain, the hurt, the betrayal, and the presumption, God reaches down into this couple's lives and heals and restores them with the privilege to carry the line of Messiah. Nothing was earned. Nothing was merited. Yet God graced them with a son, Solomon, who would become the wisest, richest, most prosperous and celebrated King in Israel's history.

Bible Reference
Matthew 1:1-16
Luke 3:23-38

Matthew records the linage of Messiah through their son Solomon right down the line to Joseph, the husband of Mary. In the gospel of Luke, we have another linage that follows David and Bathsheba's third son, Nathan, through to Mary the mother of Jesus.

God takes our failures, and he graciously weaves the story of our life into something that is not determined by the extent of our failure. Perhaps this is another aspect of David's life, that makes him a man after God's own heart. Not his human failure or the twisted corruption that followed it, but his willingness to be willing; his willingness to allow God to change his heart; his willingness to admit he was wrong, and to rely on God for restoration. His willingness to take responsibility and say sorry, his willingness to return to God and be washed clean in his forgiveness is something that God could work with.

Brennan Manning... writes this as the introduction to his book "The Furious Longing of God" [ix]*...*
"I'm Brennan. I'm an alcoholic
How I go there, why I left there, why I went back, is the story of my life.
But it is not the whole story.
I'm Brennan. I'm a Catholic.
How I got there, why I left there, why I went back, is also the story of my life.
But it is not the whole story.
I'm Brennan. I was a priest but am no longer a priest. I was a married man but am no longer a married man.
How I got to those places, why I left those places, is the story of my life too.
But it is not the whole story.
I'm Brennan. I'm a sinner saved by grace.
That is the larger and more important story.
Only God, in His fury, knows the whole of it.
Brennan Manning"

God lavishly extends the mantle of his forgiveness to include me, a sinner saved by grace. Nothing can be earned. Nothing can be merited. Nothing can disqualify me.

What is it like to remind myself that God offers generous mercy like he offered David?

Prayer:

Father God, I thank you so much for your grace on our lives. We are aware, Father God, that we are human, that we are fallible, that we don't get it right a lot of the time. We sometimes make intentional choices and sometimes we choose to try and cover up those choices. Father, forgive us for our presumption and we ask Father God, that you would wash us clean, that you would weave a story of your grace through our lives. That this grand story, the greatest story of our salvation and our restoration and our fellowship with you, Father, that this would be the dominate narrative... not our failures, but the fact that you are with us, that you are grace-full in our lives. We thank you, for your mercy and your compassion towards us. We ask Father God that we would be a people, not with hearts that are presumptive, but we would be people who will stay willing, soft before you and yield to your ways.
In Jesus name Amen.

A Humble Heart

Where we are...

We have seen what happened when David crossed some significant moral boundaries, and the consequences of those choices had lasting impacts. Sometimes there is a tendency to only reflect on the grand victories of these heroes in scripture, and notice things that have been done well and not allow for the fallibility. I don't think that actually helps me, not when I don't feel like a hero in the faith. I just feel human and flawed. But if we can notice what went wrong and how they got up again... that offers me hope.

Numbers do not always accurately tell a story. Being able to give big numbers does not always mean success. Small numbers, likewise, do not mean success or failure. Rather there is something in the heart of what is happening, that is a truer representation of what is happening. To listen to people's stories of redemption is a wonderful reminder that there is often more than what we see on the surface. It gives us a chance to hear what is in the heart. What is happening underneath what God is doing, something more than is not just about numbers.
When one of our Church executive leaders, came to our church for a meet and greet, he got a chance to hear the underneath stories; not just see the small numbers on a census report. He said to me... "It is really inspiring what God is doing here."
Today we are looking at a story in the life of David that had big numbers. Really big numbers... and it is tempting to think the big numbers represented his success, but the underneath story, was actually a very distressing example of failure.

We are going to look at another choice David made, that had even wider consequences in the life of David than what we considered in the affair with Bathsheba. But we will look at this with an open heart and see what we can learn about also holding a humble attitude, regardless of our role, positioning, or influence. We are coming to the last chapters of David's life.

As we read through the book of Second Samuel, we see fierce battles and remarkable victories of a king. After Absalom's revolt, there was another uprising against David's throne from a man from the tribe of Benjamin (King Saul's tribe) who was named Sheba. He is described as a "troublemaker". All the tribes of Israel defect over to Sheba, *except* the tribe of Judah. That's a massive split, and a tense situation in the political life of a kingdom, yet God restores the Kingdom of Israel completely to King David again.

In Chapter 21 there are a list of battles against the Philistines, and it makes special mention of men who accomplished great victories paralleled to David's stand against Goliath.

Bible Reading
2 Samuel 21:15-22

Giants Remain.

Quite literally, these Mighty Men were up against giants. These enemies were huge, gigantic warriors, all relatives of Rapha in Gath, the capital of the Philistines. Some Bible scholars believe these were the four brothers to Goliath. Gigantism runs in families, and it is possible they were related. I have heard the idea that when David chose five stones from the creek when he went out to meet Goliath, that this was a prophetic declaration in faith of victories to come. He needed only one stone for the battle against Goliath, but there were other battles to come that would be fought against his four giant warrior brothers. Whether or not that was really the case, David's army is now dealing with these remarkable opponents. These giants were skilled warriors equal to Goliath, the champion who had the whole Israeli army cowering in the time of Saul. They were huge in stature and enormously powerful in strength. The giants and problems hadn't gone away. They were still present. They still existed.

Are there giants that I am still encountering that I need courage and strength to deal with?

Courage Rises

Yet now we see that the men of Israel are not daunted when confronted with gigantic strength and overbearing intimidation. They do not cower at their taunts or their blasphemy. Now they have courage and skill, so that when they identify a gigantic problem, they can go in and address it. The heroes that are given honour by name were: Abishai, Joab's brother, the Commander of Israel's Royal army; Sibbekai; Elhanan and Jonathan, son of Shimeah, who is David's brother. So, this Jonathan was David's nephew.

Notice that David is no longer the exception, but he has set a new baseline of normal. Exceptional is becoming accepted as 'expected' rather than surprising. When one of these giant warriors from Goliath's family almost takes David out, Abishai comes in and saves David's life. He kills the giant, rescues the king, wins the war.

Who stands with me when I am tired in the battle to help me fight?

Recognition Shared

I often remember that David killed Goliath – a giant. I don't often recall that he was nearly killed by the hand of another a giant who was Goliath's relative: a very close call. David is now in his sixties. He's been fighting hard all his life; this battle was fierce, and he was getting tired. This is to be expected, but we need to remember this was never intended to be a one-man David show. He had an entire army to achieve the outcome together. That doesn't make the victory any less impressive. This act of courage put Abishai near the top of the Mighty Men list. Notice that... not right at the top but nearly. That tells us this was a seriously big list.

David makes sure that these men of valour get the recognition that they deserve. He doesn't cling to his famous Goliath victory to make others look small. There were 37 other exceptional warriors who were given the distinction of being honoured as David's Mighty Men. David shuffles across and makes room for others. That is the mark of a humble man.

Am I someone who is willing to step aside and offer recognition to those who have earned it?

But there is a situation that is recorded in both 2 Samuel 24, and, 1 Chronicles 21, that tells us that again, David did not always get it right. So, perhaps if you put a marker in both those passages, we will reference back and forth between those passages to get a fuller picture of what is difficult situation to understand. First, read the account out of Chronicles:

Bible Reading
1 Chronicles 21: 1-7
2 Samuel 24:1-9

The Census
'Incited to count'.

Right at the introduction to this account, it says Satan rose up against David and incited him to conduct a census. The parallel passage in 2 Samuel says the Lord did this.

Apparently, the literal translation from the Hebrew text does not specify a subject for the verb 'incited', so it would literally read like this:
"There was who moved David against them" or
"For one moved David against them."
Because *who* this refers to is not stated, the translators have inserted what they believe to be the intended meaning. They have taken this to mean it was God or God's anger or even Satan, who did the inciting. But there are also some other options.

The *unstated thing* that moved David to conduct the census could have been David's own idea, or his own pride or arrogance. It may have been Satan who did the inciting and God allowed it, just as God allowed Satan's hand in the example of Job or perhaps the "one" who incited David, may not have been specifically Satan, but an "adversary" which might refer to some other person such as some unnamed advisor to

David who promoted this idea and prompted him to take the census. Without researching this at a doctorate level, we know, David wanted to count, he was incited to count and there were other influences in this decision. We also know that once David got it in his head that this was a good idea, he would not be deterred. We also know it was David's responsibility, and the buck stopped with him.

Implied as pride

Joab was David's military Commander-in Chief. He is a complex character. He's good at his job. Sometimes he takes matters into his own hands; sometimes his loyalties appear to waver, and at other times he operates straight down the line. Actually – he just sounds pretty human.

In this matter of the census, Joab immediately identifies that this was not a good idea, and he tries to talk David out of this edict. *"Don't do it! I want you to prosper even more than your current circumstances, but why do you want to do this? Why should you bring guilt on Israel?"* Then the passage says, "The king's word, however, over-ruled Joab".

I can almost hear David saying: *"This is my choice. I am king and I want it done. So do it!"* This was a massive undertaking; it took nine months and twenty days to complete (2 Samuel 24:8).

Bible Reading
1 Chronicles 27:23-24

Identified as sin

Why was this census identified as sin?
Why did this stir up such a problem?
Why was Joab so distressed and repulsed by this command?

So many "Whys"!

We are not told explicitly what the issue was based on, but we have a few indications of what is going on here. David's instruction to Joab was: "Report back to me so that I may know how many there are."

Basic management would suggest it is good administration practice to know the number of people you are responsible for. There's not a problem with doing a job well, so it has to be more than that.

A consistent suggestion is that this was about David's pride and arrogance. His desire to know the extent of the vastness of the kingdom may have been vanity.

Do I remind myself that what I have, is attributed to the grace of God in my life and not just my own entitlement or cleverness?

There is also the suggestion that this was not just about the numbers. There is the idea that David was guilty of not believing that God would be true to his word to make Israel a numerous as the stars in the sky. Another idea was that he could now implement and manage a tighter taxation system that would furnish the coffers of the kingdom. Censuses are not uncommonly tied to taxation, and this would pull the Israeli people into a state of indebtedness rather than freedom. The connection to taxation is not mentioned but the counting definitely is.

In those times, a man only had the right to count or number what belonged to him[x]. Israel did not belong to David; Israel belonged to The

Lord. David was the caretaker, the custodian. It was only God's right to command a census.

In Exodus 30 there is the account where God directed Moses to conduct a census with this provision.

Bible Reference
Exodus 30:12
2 Samuel 24:10-19

David should only have conducted a census at God's command, which would have included receiving a ransom to "atone" for the counting. This is why the census was identified as a sin. It was conducted in direct conflict to what God had designated as what should happen under a Godly Kingdom, a king who reigns under God as the ultimate sovereign. His disobedience impacted David significantly.

Conscience Stricken

David is conscience stricken. After nine and a half months of this massive military manoeuvre to count the nation, David is struck with the weight of what he had done. It took him that long to get there and now the pride in his heart is humbled. His arrogance is softened, and he has a moment of clarity. He had made a big mistake. *"A very foolish thing!"*

I notice that God stays out of it until David repents. For nine and a half months The Lord is quiet but as soon as David softens his heart; as soon as he becomes repentant and asks for forgiveness, then God moves.

The very next day, the Prophet Gad is sent to David with a message. David understands that he is the shepherd. Those in his kingdom were his sheep, his responsibility. This role of shepherd wasn't something that he had left behind. This was still his mantle, to be a good shepherd, to protect and provide for those in his care. Yet his failure to be wise, affected those around him in all-pervading ways and he intercedes for his people who were innocently impacted by his unwise choices.

Our decisions and choices never just stay with us. David's choices impacted a nation. The impact went to the far reaches and the extent of his influence. If he wanted to count the people to know the extent of his influence, well now, he truly does know.

Have I considered that it is not only my successes reach to the boundaries of my influence, but also my poor choices reach there to impact other people as well?

A Choice

David had made a choice that he thought was his own to make. Now God sends Gad the Seer with another choice. I am sure I would not like to be visited by these prophets. I would not like to hear Nathan or Gad say to me, *"We need to do coffee"!*

The Prophet Gad has a word from God. David is offered 3 choices:
A famine – for 3 years.
A war – for 3 months.
A pandemic – for 3 days.

This is a selection of consequences with no win. None of them are lesser or better. How do you make such a choice? The first two options would have involved some level of dependency upon the mercy of man:

Famine would require Israel to seek relief and supplies from other nations, relying on the pity and good-will of their neighbours most of whom they had been at war with David for years.

In Chapter 21 it is recorded David has just gone through a severe famine for three years – the consequences being outworked of one of King Saul's ungodly choices. David knows what that looks like. He doesn't want to do that again.

The choice of outright Warfare, that outcome would be as severe as any pursuing enemy could dish out. I'm curious that David, who is a Warrior King, would not choose this option. He is comfortable with battlelines. That is familiar territory for him, but I suspect that David knows that in this instance, God's favour and protection would not go with him. He has been told defeat is inevitable. David can only base his decision on what he knows: and he knows the compassion of God.

He would rather throw himself on consequences coming directly from the hand of a merciful God, than rely on the fickle nature of people. That is the way he chooses to divide between a rock and a hard place. In the time of a pandemic, as disease tears through their nation, they could only look to God for relief.

When have I made a choice, but did not want to carry the responsibility for it?

Compassion in the consequences

When David had his affair with Bathsheba, he was held to account for his sin with some very significant consequences. This is the case in this instance as well. What I notice is that after the affair with Bathsheba, and the murder of her husband, the consequence, (if it is measured in human life), was that one baby died a week after he was born. This time the consequences of David's wrongdoing impacted a whole nation, 70,000 people died in three days! What David had done was extremely serious. We whisper about Bathsheba in shame, but this time, David's failure to deliver his mandate responsibly, impacted so many more on a much larger scale. The consequences are delivered in proportion to the seriousness of what happened. And yet, even then, David was correct: the compassion and mercy of God prevails. There is an atonement that was to be provided, and David obeys the word of the Lord.

David completes the instructions that God delivered through the prophet Gad. He builds an altar and humbly sacrifices burnt offerings and fellowship offerings and God's mercy prevails. The sickness is lifted.

This altar was built on a threshing floor belonging to Araunah (A-raw-nah) the Jebusite. A Jebusite was someone who was a native of Jerusalem. Jerusalem traditionally was called both Jebus and Salem. So, in the place that is called the city of Peace, and the City of David, on the place that was a threshing floor, where the harvested grain was beaten and winnowed and separated from the chaff... an altar of atonement was built.

Bible Reference
Matthew 3:11-12

What echoes of Messiah can we notice here?

John the Baptist, under the unction of the Holy Spirit said this about Messiah, even before he even knew that Jesus was that person. John spoke of Messiah with these two parallel elements of water and fire. Purifying and cleansing. Washing and burning. They seem completely opposed. Yet here on this threshing floor, as David builds an altar of atonement, there is a prophetic echo of a Messiah who holds a winnowing fork.

A Messiah who will clear his threshing floor.
A Messiah who will gather the wheat harvest to himself.
A Messiah who will purify with fire, not just for the harvest, to burn the chaff... but like the bush of Moses, with a fire that will not be put out.

This is what David needed. This is what the nation of Israel needed: Purifying and cleansing. As we conclude our series on David with one final reflection, we will explore more about how the compassionate mercy of God is shown from this very same threshing floor.

David wrote Psalm 18 as he was fleeing from Saul. This was a prayer full of a truth that he needs to hold onto in this situation. The truth is that God is faithful. God's justice and judgements are sure. This is real, even when David is on the other side of the judgement seat and not standing before it as one who is innocent.

Bible Reading
Psalm 18

David is fully dependent on God's mercy. God, the One who saves the humble, brings low those whose eyes are haughty. 'God, your Way is perfect, your Word is flawless,' he prays. Without God's great mercy, restoration, cleansing and purifying, David's life was not notable. There is a reminder in this prayer to protect a humble heart. Yes, David did become the head of nations. People, he did not even know, now served him. Yes – his heart got off course, yet God in his grace steers him back to genuine truth. That is the sober reminder of the mercy in this story.

Final Thoughts...

This story is another example of where David gets off track... really off track! And the consequences of his choice are devastating and wide sweeping.

John Newton's story, the man who penned Amazing Grace, is well known:
He had a believing mother, and unbelieving father. He became a sailor; deserted ship; was flogged; became a slave; escaped; became a slave trader; was saved; became a pastor for 20 years and was a champion of Wilberforce to help abolish slavery in the British Empire. He wrote the famous hymn: 'Amazing Grace'.
In fact, Newton wrote many poems and hymns. It is said that he usually finished his sermons with a new poem every week. After 20 years, that's a lot of poetry. Someone suggested this was a great idea for every pastor to finish their messages in this way. That's an unusual challenge, and I am certain it is not everyone's style! From Newton's prolific works, he often wrote on the theme of God's grace:

"Cheer up, my soul, there is a mercy seat,
Sprinkled with blood, where Jesus answers prayer;
There humbly cast thyself beneath his feet,
For never needy sinner perished there.
Lord, give me faith--he hears! what grace is this
Dry up thy tears, my soul, and cease to grieve;
He shows me what he did, and who he is,
I must, I will, I can, I do believe."

That is a voice that speaks from experience. God takes our failures, and sometimes we have to live out the consequences of our choices. Yet still, in his mercy, God provides a way of atonement and grace. We know that there is atonement for us, at the mercy seat. Jesus is our risen saviour, who saves us from ourselves, and our flawed choices. He is the Messiah of the threshing floor, who sacrificed himself as a way for us to be restored.

David humbly acknowledges the extent of his failure. He throws himself on God's amazing grace. He allowed God to be the bearer of his consequences; he relies on God for his restoration and the restoration of those who impacted by what he had done. He was willing to be washed clean in God's forgiveness and go through the fire of God's purification.

Prayer:

Father God, in many respects, this is a very difficult story, but we hang onto the idea that there is a mercy seat, and there is a God who answers our prayer. We thank you that you are a God who can take failure and turn it around and restore us into a whole life, a new life, a grace filled life! Father, we thank you that you see every part of us, and we ask Father God that you will help us to protect our own heart before you.

Help us so that we would not be pride-filled, we would not be independent, we would not like to know the all the big numbers that make us look good, but rather that we would stay soft and humble before you. What we have is through your own grace and generosity. Father, help us to be people who can shuffle aside and make room for others to be acknowledged and honoured. We thank you for your goodness to us. We thank you that you are a good God, an honourable God, a loving God, a merciful God and we ask Father that in all of the things that we need to do, as life happens, that you will help us to be carriers of that humility into our families, our workplaces, into our neighbourhood and friendship groups.

We ask this in Jesus' name. Amen.

11

A Prophetic Heart

Where we are...

We have witnessed David cross a significant line of responsibility before God when he called a census throughout the nation of Israel. The consequences of that choice had wide-spreading impacts. Yet we also saw that God provided a way so that restitution and reconciliation could be made from what David confessed was "a very foolish thing..."

We are concluding our journey through the life of David, and what the Holy Spirit imparts to him prophetically was not just a small word of encouragement, but many, many profound and intricate details that he wrote down. Those things would impact generations and generations of people around the world, down through the ages.

One day we were out for lunch... and the friend we were sharing the meal with, looked at me and said, "You have a lot of stories inside of you. You need to write them down."
It was said so normally. Almost in passing, and I knew this man didn't know I had been writing stories at all, because it had been an on-and-off private hobby for many, many years. But I also felt that what he had said was spoken prophetically and was part of the encouragement God gave me to take what was in my heart, and write it down, even if, at that stage, I could not see if anyone else would participate in those stories that I had inside of me.

Redemption

Bible Reference
Genesis 22:2, 13-14

The Threshing floor of Araunah the Jebusite was the specific place where Gad had told David to build an altar to the Lord and offer sacrifices.

Where is my Threshing Floor - the place where I recognised the grace and power of God in my life?

The location of this threshing floor was historically significant. This was the same mountain, Mount Moriah, where Abraham was led to worship the Lord and where God provided a substitute sacrifice for his son Isaac.

David rightly identified that he could not offer a sacrifice, that costs him nothing. That would neutralize the 'sacrifice' part. So, he pays Araunah for the land, builds an altar on the threshing floor and offers sacrifices there. It is here that David witnesses the redemption of the Lord. It is here that we see God wipes away the guilt of his sin. It is here that we see God intervenes against the consequences of his choices. It is here that we see God meets with David in a powerful way. Not just through the visitation of the Commander Angel with the sword, but fire falls from heaven and consumes the sacrifice that David offered. This was a powerful demonstration that God had accepted this sacrifice.

We see God has supernaturally ignited sacrifices of his people in significant times in scripture before this:

Bible Reference
Genesis 15:17

When God made a covenant with Abraham. Abraham laid out divided sacrifices to The Lord, and God sealed the covenant with fire that consumed the sacrifice with fire from a firepot and a blazing torch.

Bible Reference
Leviticus 9:24

It happens again when Aaron offered the first sacrifices in the Tabernacle that they built as they were coming out of slavery in Egypt. Aaron had performed the sacrifices to The Lord, and God sealed that offering with fire that came out of his presence and consumed the sacrifice. A covenant was sealed between God and Israel.

Here we see the same powerful display of God's redemption and acceptance of David's sacrifice as fire falls from the sky and consumes his sacrifice.

Reverence

There is a heightened sense of reverence as David meets God in this place. David is not a man who took God lightly at any time. His life has been punctuated with praise, and worship, and prayers of repentance, and humility, and commitment to God and his ways. Yet here we see the reverence in which David holds his relationship with God go up. And it did not go up just a notch or two, but rockets through the roof. His reverence before God is now incredibly profound. God is holy, awesome and powerful. He is a God of great and frightening deeds, as well as the God of compassion and kindness. This is the Great God that David now sees revealed.

How do I show my profound reverence... not only of the generous grace of God in my life, but also his power and sovereignty?

Revealed the location of the temple

The kindness David now experiences from God means that something that has been on his heart for a long, long time, is starting to be stirred again. Ever since David brought the Ark of the covenant into Jerusalem, he had something on his heart that he wanted to do. He spoke to Nathan the prophet and unveiled his desire to build a proper temple for God, so that the Ark was not just residing in a tent.

Bible Reading
2 Samuel 7:1-13

David wanted to build God 'a proper' temple for the Ark to dwell in, but God says, "No."
Really? "No?"

Bible Reference
Psalm 36:4-5

In Psalm 37:4-5 David writes these words...
"Delight yourself in the LORD; and he shall give you the desires of thine heart. Commit your way to the LORD; trust also in him; and he shall bring it to pass."

I've seen these verses used like an incantation, a magic wand. The idea promotes the idea that if I want it; if I desire it; I can have it; my desire will be manifested; because it's written in the Bible; God will give me the desires of my heart.

However, if I take this approach and it happens that I don't get what I want, in some way that seems to be used to invalidate the sovereignty of God and his Word. Sometimes, it is explained like this: God will plant desires in our heart and then we will be given *those* things. God given things.

Are there desires in my heart that I haven't seen fulfilled?

Yet, here we see that David's heart was to build God a temple, an appropriately opulent and glorious place to hold the Ark of the Covenant, a beautiful place for the magnificent presence of God to be worshiped. David loved God. David delighted in the Lord. David wanted the people of the nations to acknowledge God's greatness. He wanted to spread the honour of God's name. This was the desire of his heart: a good heart, a good desire and I would suggest even a desire planted there by the Holy Spirit.

So, what we see is that sometimes, even when those desires are coming out of a good place, an honourable place, a God-breathed place...we still notice, that God, in his sovereignty, might say... "No, this is not for you."

Sometimes, when this happens, God is not withholding it from us... but trusting us to hold it *in trust* for someone coming after us. We can pray prophetically into this desire. We can see it with the eyes of faith and still believe for it. This is what we see that God does with David's desire. David never gets to see this particular desire fulfilled; he never walks through those beautiful temple colonnades of the Temple courts himself, but he now knows *where* this temple will be built. He knows that this good desire will come to pass. He knows God will make sure that it comes to pass, right where he is standing on the Threshing Floor of Araunah, on Mount Moriah.

This is where his son would build the Temple of God. The place of atonement is where the foundations of God's house would be made. This Temple would usher, not just David and his family, but generations of Israelites, into the presence of God in worship.

So, what does David do with this knowledge?

Bible Reading
1 Chronicles 22: 2-5; 8-10

Part of Preparations is defining our Role

David had been a Warrior-King. That was his role. He fought battle after battle after battle. He was a king who fought for peace, but did not completely experience peace himself. Still, he invested wholeheartedly in pursuing it. This meant he was a man who shed blood, a lot of blood. He did his job well, but it also meant that he was not the right person for this next commission.

God wanted his house to be built as a house of peace, not war. David's response is, "Okay God... I will not get to do this, but *"I will make preparations for it!"* David now understands his role in this. To set it up and make it ready to go. There is no pouting; no sense that he felt this was not fair, or that he was missing out. David didn't go ahead and try and build it anyway, but he makes a resolution in his heart, to get ready for everything that was needed to see this desire and vision become a reality.

Plans Revealed

The temple is known throughout history as Solomon's Temple, but we know that God gave the blueprint of the plans to David. God gave David the large concept. God gave him the small details. David gets the whole download from the Holy Spirit. Not just architectural plans, but also the finishes, the furnishings, the articles of worship. It wasn't just the physical aspects of the temple that the Holy Spirit imparted to David. God also clarified the processes and procedures that were needed for the Levites, gatekeepers and musicians. How would the practises that were handed down by Moses for the Tabernacle, now be translated into the Temple? Their place of worship would no longer be a portable tent, but a solid structure built on a solid foundation. God shows David how it will all look, and he writes it all down.

Resources compiled

Absalom, when he was king for a short time, built monuments to himself because he had no children. What I like about this part of David's story is that he is so willing to resource this incredible project without apology, or without trying to make it his legacy for the generations to come. This project was not David's attempt at a monument or a legacy. David always is clear that this is God's temple first and foremost. And still David works to resource this plan so thoroughly, so extravagantly.

David stockpiles dressed masonry; he accumulates gold, silver, iron and bronze. Beautiful timbers. He imported cedar of the best quality. God has literally given him the plans in extraordinary detail, and David gets behind it completely. His invests in stock-piling the rich resources needed for this prophetic vision to be accomplished.

Have I been charged with a trust that I have started, but not yet completed?

How far has David come, now that he is at the end of his life? We have witnessed him from a young shepherd boy who at the age of fifteen was out in the paddock, not even acknowledged by his father as one of his sons. And then, when it is time to pass the baton on, David charges Solomon, his own son, who has been crowned as the next king of Israel, to take the lead on managing this project and he passes this trusted commission over into the hand of his son.

Bible Reading
2 Chronicles 28:9-21

Charged with a trust

David charges his son Solomon, not only as king with the crown and the throne, but with the trust of fulfilling the building The Lord's beautiful temple. Every detail has been provided and recorded. Every resource has been provided and catalogued.

Courage to start

David prays for Solomon, that he would have the courage to start this rather overwhelming project. "Be strong and courageous" he prays. This was the same prayer that was spoken over Joshua, six times as he was taking new ground when occupying the promised land.
"Be strong and courageous!"

This sounds like a warrior's prayer, a fighting prayer, "strong and courageous" like Joshua, or David. It seems a strange prayer to offer up for a man of peace, but I think David understands this is also taking new ground. This was establishing something that had not been done before. This is the way of the Kingdom of God; this temple was a signpost to God, and a prophetic signpost to Messiah and it would not happen without resistance, or distraction, or issues, or push-back. Such a big project could seem overwhelming. Be courageous.

Continue to the end

Don't be discouraged: keep going, right to the end. Keep going right up until it is finished. It is one thing to start, it is another thing to finish and this was a project that needed to be finished.

What do I need to do to keep going with what God has given me to do until it is finished?

It was so important that this was to be completed in the way that God had designed it, exactly as the Holy Spirit had given these plans to David. The temple, just like the tabernacle, was a prophetic signpost to Messiah. At the Last Supper, Jesus made this declaration:
"I am the way and the truth and the life. No man comes to the Father except through me." (John 14:6).

This was a declaration – not just about how our relationship with Jesus provides direction (The way), or discernment (the truth), or fulfilment (the life). This was a direct reference to the prophetic vision of the Temple[xi].
    The gate into the outer court was called "The Way".
    The gate into the inner court was called "The Truth".
    The gate into the Holy of Holies was called "The Life".

No one comes to the Father except through Jesus Christ – Messiah the One who is the Way to the Father; Jesus Christ – Messiah who is the revealed Truth of the Father; Jesus Christ – Messiah who gives us access to Life with the Father.

If the gates of the temple offer increasing level of intimacy with my relationship with God... which court, am I standing in? The outer court? The inner court? Or the Holy of Holies?

The Temple was a prophetic declaration that the Messiah would come from the Lineage and House of David, not just in the genealogy that we have recorded in the gospels, but in the very nature of what the Holy Spirit revealed in the pattern provided in the Temple.

The template of the Temple, in all of its magnificence, was a foretaste of a more profound, more intimate relationship that is available to us, right into the Holy of Holies through Jesus Christ, the gateway of Life.

When David had handed over the patterns and plans and diagrams and the order of procedures of the temple to Solomon, he offered this heart-felt prayer in front of all the dignitaries and heads of the tribes who were gathered.

Bible Reading
1 Chronicles 29:10-20

So, all the people praised the LORD, the God of their fathers; they bowed down, prostrating themselves before the LORD and the king. David has a full heart as he hands the baton over to his son Solomon.

Final Thoughts...

This account is a beautiful conclusion to our journey with David. It is not only a high point in a life lived well, but it is also aligned with the heart of a man who has journeyed life with God. There is a fruitfulness in this picture of a man who holds up a torch for the next generation to carry and complete the good work that God started in him and through him. By the Holy Spirit, David prophetically is given the plans and drawings for the Temple. But it is more than just a building that he sees, it is our relationship with God which is ultimately fulfilled through Messiah.

Bible Reading
John 10:9-11

Jesus is Messiah who is represented in the gates of the Temple. Messiah himself is the Way, the Truth and the Life, the passage for us to be restored into relationship with Father God. I think it is rather meaningful that at another time, Jesus refers to himself as the gate, and that was in reference to being called the Good Shepherd.

My father once was conducting a funeral for a friend, whose family were not people of faith. My father gave a family member a 'Poem' to read during the service. She spoke to him afterwards and shared how this beautiful poem had really moved her. She wondered where he had found it.
It was the 23rd Psalm....
"The Lord is my Shepherd; I shall not want...".
This is the profound impact of words breathed on by the Holy Spirit, that continue to touch our souls, whether we know the Good Shepherd or not...

I wanted to finish this series by reading the 23rd Psalm. I don't think we can we look at the story of David and not have this psalm as part of our journey. It would be good if you could read it from a modern translation that is not familiar, as the beauty of the imagery can sometimes be refreshed by listening to a different rhythm of words.

Bible Reading – The Message version is suggested
Psalm 23

What part of this Psalm refreshes my soul?

The words of David continue to impact us... as they prophetically point to Jesus, the good shepherd. I think this song, in a beautiful way, represents the circle of David's life. It starts in the pastures and finishes in the House of God. It finishes with a feast and a cup brimming with blessing.

Prayer:

Father God, our cup brims with your blessings, and we thank you that we can stand in the courts of your house and declare your praises. We thank you God, that it is not through the process of sacrifice but through your son Jesus, who is the Way and the Truth and the Life, that we have the privilege to participate in fellowship with you. Father, we thank you so much that you have called us your own children. We thank you that we have the story of David recorded for us so that we may reflect over some of these things that have impacted his life, generations of Jews down history and your people from across the globe. Father, I pray that as we close this story of David there are things that you may plant in our heart, prophetic things that you may use to speak into our life.

May we be people who follow you as the good shepherd, so that we may know and listen to your voice and be discerning in the things that you have called us to participate in.

We ask these things in the precious name of Jesus, our Good Shepherd. Amen.

Other books in this Series

Endnotes

[i] https://www.chabad.org/theJewishWoman/article_cdo/aid/280331/jewish/Nitzevet-Mother-of-David.htm

[ii] https://weis.bibleodyssey.com/articles/psalm-151-and-the-dead-sea-scrolls/

[iii] https://kuyperian.com/kill-goliath-and-save-his-skull/#:~:text=For%20the%20very%20place%20that,is%20to%20be%20crucified%3A%20Golgotha.&text=As%20James%20B.,Hebrew%3A%20Goliath%2DGath).

[iv] https://judaism.stackexchange.com/questions/35330/abigails-thigh

[v] Complete Works of Josephus, Antiquities of the Jews; Book VII, Chapter 5; section 5.

[vi] R. T. Kendall in https://www.premierchristianity.com/christian-living/rt-kendall-heres-what-my-finest-hour-will-look-like/18081.article

[vii] C. S. Lewis, Mere Christianity

[viii] https://www.gotquestions.org/wives-King-David.html

[ix] Brennan Manning, The Furious Longing of God.

[x] https://www.gotquestions.org/David-census.html

[xi] https://emmausroadministries.international/2020/02/08/the-way-the-truth-and-the-life-tabernacle-series-part-4/

www.ingramcontent.com/pod-product-compliance
Lightning Source LLC
Chambersburg PA
CBHW061219070526
44584CB00029B/3904